W9-BKE-930

RACING FOR RECOVERY

RACING FOR RECOVERY

From Addict to Ironman

Todd Crandell and John Hanc

BREAKAWAY BOOKS
HALCOTTSVILLE, NEW YORK
2006

Racing for Recovery: From Addict to Ironman
Copyright 2006 by Todd Crandell and John Hanc

ISBN: 1-891369-61-X
ISBN-13: 978-1-891369-61-2
Library of Congress Control Number: 2005938237

"Ironman" and "Ironman Triathlon" are registered trademarks of the World Triathlon Corporation
and are used in this title by permission.

Published by Breakaway Books
P.O. Box 24
Halcottsville, NY 12438
(800) 548-4348
www.breakawaybooks.com

10 9 8 7 6 5 4 3

Contents

ACKNOWLEDGMENTS

The authors would like to thank Garth Battista for believing in this book; and Jim Cooper, Robert Spina, Jr., Kathleen Hannan, and Dr. Steven Jonas for their invaluable contributions to the project.

Todd Crandell would like to thank the following for making this book possible: God; my beautiful wife, Melissa; my amazing kids Skylar, Konor, Madison, and Mason; my parents, Terry and Cindy; my brother Jason; my birth mother Louise; my Grandmother Lillian Ward and the rest of my family. Thanks to my friends who have stuck by me and put up with my behaviors both good and bad over the years. Thanks also to my personal triathlon coach, Scott Horns; my attorneys John Fisher, Rick Martin, and Jenifer Belt for your legal counsel; Stephanie Calmes, Jenifer Skelding, and Brian "Monk" Taylor; COMPASS drug treatment center and Whitmer High School for giving me my public speaking start, the Racing for Recovery Board of Directors, and to all of the race directors, athletes, schools, churches, and business groups who have allowed me to share my message. Special thanks to Kenny and Anne Marie from 3Disciplines Racing and Aaron Haydu from Inside-In Design for donating their services. My heartfelt thanks also goes to those individuals who have written me, prayed for me, or who shook my hand or raced with me in support of my recovery.

John Hanc would also like to thank: Linda Konner for her guidance in shaping and directing this project in its early stages; Lee Schreiber for his wise counsel; the academic grant committee at New York Institute of Technology, for giving me the time to pursue this project; Barbara Schuler and Margaret Corvini, features editors at *Newsday* who assigned and edited my story on Todd that first brought us together, and above all to my wife—and first reader—Donna, and son, Andrew, for their love and unwavering support.

This book was written for the dreamers and believers. For the people who have struggled or are still struggling with an addiction that has ruined their life and hurt those who love them.

It is an expression of insecurity, anger, frustration, pain, recovery, perseverance, humility, gratitude, happiness, and the will to overcome—and to inspire others to improve their lives.

To those who said I would never achieve this and I was wasting my time for trying: I hope you find compassion and faith in all you pursue.

Introduction

My legs felt like rubber as I stumbled down the road. I was nauseous, dizzy, a little disoriented. Pain seemed to radiate from every part of my body. My friends and family had warned me; they told me that I was hurting myself by doing this, but I ignored them. I had to do this. It meant so much to me, in fact, that I would do anything to achieve it. As the puffy clouds in the blue Florida sky began to circle my fevered head, I gritted my teeth, determined that I could tolerate the agony for just a little while longer. Because very shortly I was going to feel really, really good.

God, it was great to be off drugs and alcohol!

The last few miles of the Ironman Triathlon were excruciating but next to my wedding and the births of my children, this was the greatest day of my life. If my rubber legs, vacant expression, and fuzzy mind were symptoms I had experienced before—in another, darker life—this time they were not due to wanton ingestion of outrageous amounts of illegal substances. No, on this day, November 6, 1999, I was about to become a member of an elite group; one of the few people in the world—probably less than fifty thousand—who can say that they have finished an Ironman.

The term gets thrown around a lot, but do you know what the Ironman event really is? It's a triathlon consisting of a 2.4-mile swim, a 112-mile bike ride and *then* a marathon—a 26.2-mile run to be exact. "You do it on three consecutive days?" a friend asked me when he first heard about this. No—you do them on the same day, one right after the other.

This Ironman was being held in Panama City, Florida. With seventeen hundred competitors, it's one of the biggest on the East Coast. After fourteen hours, I was now nearing the finish line—it was the end, not only of a ridiculously long race and a grueling six-month training period. It was also the completion of my long walk into sunlight: the clear skies of almost seven years of sobriety, a new life, a new purpose. With my wife, Melissa, cheering and waving a GO TODD sign, I crossed the line with a big smile and a few tears glistening in my eyes. Then somebody draped a finisher's medal around my neck. Damn, I did it. I did it!

This, the greatest day in my life, would stand in stark contrast with another day in another part of Florida—when I was another person, an addicted person. What I did then was nothing to be proud of.

It was Christmas 1986. I sat alone on the sand at Cocoa Beach, Florida, sipping from a bottle of cheap vodka. I was nineteen years old, and I had been kicked off my team, kicked out of school, kicked out of my parents' house. That last time I kicked back: Just two months earlier, I had beat the shit out of my parents. Yes, a lot of stuff had come to a head about my dad and my stepmother and one night, while I was trying to do what I usually did—get as fucked up as I could, and get laid as often as I could—my dad came in. He saw Jenny—I wasn't allowed to have girlfriends in the house. He was angry that I'd blown off work for another day, and on top of it all I had just gotten my first tattoo. He was pissed as hell. I was stoned out of my mind. We were screaming at each other, and my step-mom cames in. She saw the girlfriend and started to physically pull her out of the room, presumably to get her out of the line of fire. Something exploded inside my highly combustible head. I turned around, punched my stepmom in the head, and then shoved her. She went flying into a shelf full of my old hockey trophies—they fell and shattered on the floor, an apt metaphor for my life at that point. I then grabbed her head and gave her some uppercuts to her head and stomach.

Then when my dad came to her aid, I took him and threw him into my closet. I grabbed Jenny, and we ran out of the house. My parents, who—thank God—were not hurt seriously, never pressed charges, although it didn't matter. I was already looking at an eight-year prison term for receiving stolen property. Although I never ended up serving that sentence, there were still a good thirty-three days ahead of me spent in the warm confines of a jail cell somewhere.

That night in Florida two months later, I thought about all this, and just drank more. Finally I passed out underneath an air conditioner hanging out the window of some fleabag hotel. When I woke up a necklace I wore had been stolen by some bums—torn off my neck, and I hadn't felt a thing, I was so looped. I was alone, broke, stoned, miserable. That day, I opened a card my parents had sent me (it wasn't until I became a parent that I could understand how they could possibly send a holiday card to a son who had physically assaulted them barely two months earlier).

"Remember Christmas past," the card said on the front. Then I opened it up and read, "Because this is your Christmas present." And there was an elf holding a candle and that was it. *Yeah,* I remember thinking. *That's my life, in a damn greeting card: bad past, worse present, and definitely no future.*

I was wrong about that last part.

I'm now thirty-nine years old and I'm still an addict. But I've been sober since April 15, 1993. Over the course of a thirteen-year battle with alcohol and drugs, I nearly killed myself and a few other people. I lost everything I had—my family, a promising sports career, my self-respect, and yes, nearly my life. I had a gun in my mouth and a foot in the grave. I was in jail and I was in deep shit.

I was a strong, macho guy who was ultimately brought to his knees by drugs and alcohol. At the last possible minute I made a screeching U-turn in my life. And I kept going in the other direction—past sobriety, right through the rebuilt version of my life and into what some might call a healthier addiction: the Ironman triathlon. Although few people can actually complete one, it's one of the hottest endurance sports in America. The Ironman Triathlon World Championship, held every October in Hawaii, is one of the most popular annual sports broadcasts on NBC.

Through a nationwide series of road races and triathlons, I raise money for my foundation, Racing for Recovery, which promotes substance abuse education and prevention. In my regular speaking and media engagements—about one a week, from local junior high schools to national media—I tell kids and adults and people who are like me or are trying to become like me what it's all about: what it's like to be completely over-powered by alcohol and drugs, and what it's like to regroup, rally, and counterattack, to seize back control of your life.

I always get an enormous response. I'd like to think it's my wit, charm, and funny jokes that do it, but the truth is that my story resonates with so many people because the essence of it is all too familiar to so many families.

Let's face it, we're a nation of addicts: We're addicted to fast food, reality TV, cell phones, credit cards, Starbucks, Vegas, Viagra. Excessive use of any of the aforementioned can cause problems, but nothing like the kind of problems we face through drug and alcohol addiction: According to the Department of Health and Human Services, an estimated twenty-two million Americans—9.4 percent of the popula-tion ages twelve and over—are classified with substance dependence or abuse. Those substances include, of course, illicit drugs, such as marijuana and cocaine (19.5 million Americans use such drugs); alcohol (15.9 million Americans are classified as "heavy users"); and prescription drugs, which, when put into the hands of an addict, can be just as destruc-tive as the illegal ones (as Rush Limbaugh proved).

The effect of this behavior on the individuals, their families and friends—and on our society—is almost incalculable. Consider these statistics from the National Institute on Drug Abuse:

—Every thirty minutes someone in the United States is killed in an alcohol-related traffic accident.

—The fourth leading cause of death among people ages ten through twenty-four is alcohol, and alcohol and drug abuse are major factors in the first three (suicide, motor vehicle crashes, and homicide).

—Nearly 1.5 million arrests for drug abuse are made each year.

—Four out of ten criminal offenders report alcohol as a factor in violence; it's also involved in one of out three incidents of spousal violence.

—According to the National Council on Alcoholism and Drug Dependence, alcohol and drug abuse cost the American economy an estimated $276 billion per year in lost productivity, health care expenditures, crime, motor vehicle crashes and other problems.

Clearly, millions of people in this country are affected by these addictions. They lurk in every corner of American society—from the stereotypical heroin junkie shooting up in an alley; to high school students hiding their coke habits from their parents; to the lawyer or physician or business owner gulping down martinis or Valium to get through the day.

Horrifying as these numbers are, I don't see the problem as abstract statistics: I see real people, with real problems. In my weekly drug support group meetings, through my foundation, and during my frequent speaking engagements at schools, businesses, and other organizations, I see people like Kyle, Warren, Jenna, Jim—or their parents or friends or loved ones—and I try to give them hope and something to hang on to. I tell them about how instead of dying, I'm really living now . . . maybe for the first time. I own my own house in the suburbs. I've got a wonderful wife and four beautiful kids. I've got a purpose in life and it's to make sure that fewer people follow in the sodden footprints I left as I muddied up the first half of my life.

And, boy, did I muddy it up. I was a guy blessed with just about every advantage you could think. I grew up in a nice upper-middle-class community; my dad had a successful business. I was fortunate enough to possess athletic talent, some smarts, and, so I'm told, good looks. Yeah, I had it all, but because I was cursed with something else—a genetic predisposition toward alcoholism and my own emotional problems, stupidity, and bad judgment—I lost it all. Kicked off the team. Kicked out of school. Fights. Jail. Homelessness. Attempted suicide. Lots of depraved and hair-raising incidents that, if you've battled addiction or know someone who has, you can relate to. Some of them are almost funny, in a sick way, such as the time I went out and got drunk in Ohio and woke up in Georgia. My life was like the old party-hearty anthem stuck on a scratch in a vinyl record: "Sex, drugs, drugs, drugs, drugs, drugs . . . vrrrrppp . . . and rock and roll."

In short, I would do anything to anybody in order to get what I needed—and what I needed was to get high. Really high, all the time—on whatever I could get my hands on. Some addicts specialize. I'm a generalist, and I took a perversely democratic view toward drugs and alcohol. If it could mess me up, I was all for taking it . . . lots and lots of it: Booze. Weed. Coke snorted or the smoked variety, crack. Valium. Good drugs, bad drugs, they were all welcome to go flying up my nose or down my gullet.

But here's where my story changes. Through a lot of hard work and support from a lot of people, and a little luck, I got my life back—and then some. Now my world is built around my family, my training and fitness and athletic competition, and my work in helping to educate and prevent drug abuse, among kids and adults.

That day in Florida, as I stumbled along sore-legged and dehydrated, was truly one of the great moments of my life—and one of the best highs. And what was really sweet about it was that this time it was achieved without any substance more potent than Gatorade.

People say they find my story "inspiring." Well, you'll be the judge of that. I don't hold myself up as some kind of role model for what I did in the first half of my life; but the fact that I was able to turn things around when they were really bad—and as you'll see, they were *really* bad—would suggest that others can, too. Maybe you're someone who has battled addiction, as I did. Maybe you've watched a close friend or loved one deal with the disease. Or perhaps you'd just like to hear a story with a happy ending. Heaven knows, there aren't all that many in the world these days.

Regardless of your motivation in picking up my book, I invite you to follow in my footsteps—not necessarily through the 140 total miles covered in an Ironman, but into an understanding that with hope, with sobriety, with determination, there is a better life for all of us.

1

Route 23 and the Roots of Addiction

Terry and Louise Crandell never should have had children.

It's a tough thing for me to admit, as I am the sole progeny of their brief and turbulent marriage, but that is the truth. Terry Crandell, my dad, was nineteen. He had just finished his freshman year at Ohio State University and was home working with his dad in the family business. Louise, my mom, was sixteen and still in high school. They met at a local swimming hole, a common gathering place for Midwest kids who don't have ocean beaches to go to. She was blonde and pretty. He was blond and handsome. A real all-American couple from the heartland. Or so it appeared.

I suspect in retrospect Louise Swab was looking for someone

to rescue her, and Dad came along just at the right time. Her own father, Richard Swab, was a real cold fish, a disciplinarian. Years later, as a child going with my dad to visit his wife's parents, I spilled some milk in my grandfather's presence at the dinner table. I'll never forget the look in his eye; like he wanted to kill me. On the way home that night, I told my dad I never wanted to go there again. We didn't.

Terry and Louise started getting hot and heavy at the quarry. So much so that Terry decided against returning to Ohio State University, the first of many questionable decisions he was making back then. After three years of dating, they decided it was time to get married. That's the official version, at least. The truth is, she'd been shacking up with him and had become pregnant with me, so they had to get hitched or ol' Grandpa Swab would have come after my dad with a shotgun.

It was not an auspicious way to start a marriage.

My mom had a wild streak. Not surprising, considering that their whole generation was going wild. This was the 1960s, and they were both right in the middle of it. Dad smoked some pot, but rarely drank. That didn't stop Mom. In addition to smoking weed and drinking heavily, she did coke, took speed, and eventually became addicted to heroin. She was shooting up not only in the little house that she and Terry moved into but in her dad's house, as well. Now, that took some cojones, to be fixing in her bedroom while old disciplinarian Dad was lurking around in the living room looking for something to piss him off!

On top of this, she had a kid to take care of. I was born on December 12, 1966. Mom was nineteen, Dad twenty-two. The first two years went well but the wheels started to come of the baby buggy when Louise wanted to party once in a while with her single friends. Being the Sixties, those old friends introduced her to some new friends: Marijuana, LSD, mescaline and speed, and eventually heroin, to which she soon became addicted. The more time she spent with her new friends the less time she wanted to stay married.

I don't think my dad realized how far things had gotten so quickly, until the time he came home to find a dealer in the house, angry over having not been paid, waving a gun around and threatening to shoot both his wife and baby son. Terry calmed the guy down and gave him some money, and he left. But that was the breaking point. Louise could no longer hide her addiction—or the fact that she had made yet another friend, this one male, and fallen in love with him. Terry and Louise were headed for splitsville. Terry got custody of me, until she could get clean.

She tried, but I don't think she ever really did. Besides, she was hot and heavy with lover boy. Pregnant, apparently—a smart move considering that she couldn't even take care of one kid and one man, let alone two of each. My dad, who wanted his wife to regain control of her life and come back home, tried to support her. There was talk of her getting an abortion, but she was afraid; a friend of hers had died while getting one.

Then, the breaking point: Late in the summer of 1970, her boyfriend—I don't even know his name—was killed in a car accident. We don't know for sure, but we figure that Louise must have snapped over this. She was dealing with a lot of conflicting emotions—about taking care of me, about her failed relationship, about her family, about being pregnant, about her drug use, and about her feelings for this guy—and his death must have put her over the edge.

About a week later, on the night of September 23, 1970, she got into her black 1969 Bonneville. It had rained that day, but the roads weren't wet by the time she went out, which was late at night. She headed out on Route 23, the road between Ohio and Michigan. Right on the state line, she crashed into a concrete abutment. No one saw her. There was no one else on that stretch of the road at the time. Based on the autopsy, she wasn't intoxicated at the time.

My mom's death was ruled a suicide; the first vehicular suicide in Ohio state history.

Louise never wanted a big funeral, so I'm told. But her parents did. And at the end of it, old Grandpa Swab handed my dad the bill. Guess he figured he knew who to blame for her death. Couldn't be the repressive household she grew up in; couldn't be his nasty demeanor; couldn't be any number of factors . . . no, it was all Terry's fault.

Louise was gone, her unborn child was gone, and before long, so was her family. Grandpa Swab died a few years later. Louise's sister died of diabetes that was not helped by her obesity, which she refused to do anything about. Her brother, apparently a huge acidhead during his days at OSU, also committed suicide. The only ones left were another sister, whom we lost track of, and my grandmother Swab, who retired to Florida after her husband's death. When I showed up at her door in Florida in 1985, she spoke to me for fifteen or twenty minutes and then politely asked me to leave. In a sense, I don't blame her. I was probably a reminder of a terrible tragedy in her life: the loss of her daughter. She chose to erase me from her life, the way you might delete an unwanted or unpleasant e-mail today.

In retrospect, the fact that both my mother and her brother had drug problems should have been a huge, red flashing warning signal in the rearview window of my life. But at the time, no one thought about that. They—Terry, her parents, the rest of our family and friends—wanted to put it all behind them as quickly as possible, and so Louise ceased to exist, in memory as well as in substance; written out of our history books, like some nonperson in Soviet Russia, for the next decade.

In the years since, I've met a lot of addicts who came from family situations like mine, and much worse. Abusive parents, absent parents, suicidal parents, screwball parents. I've also met addicts who came from perfectly normal homes. Either way, at some point what your parents did or didn't do ceases to be an excuse for your drug addiction or alcoholism—or for any other behavior in your life, for that matter. That said, it would be foolish to think that having a mother I don't remember, a mother who was addicted to drugs, a mother who committed suicide, didn't have an effect on me. It most surely did.

But it wasn't the only reason I became an addict.

To fully understand Terry and Louise Crandell, to understand me—and everything that happened afterward—you have to understand Sylvania. This is the town where Mom and Dad grew up and met. This is the town where I was born and raised hell, and it's where I still choose to live. Let me give you a little tour.

Sylvania is a suburb of Toledo, in the northwestern corner of Ohio, just a few miles from the Michigan border. The closest major city is Detroit, sixty miles to the north.

The town was founded in 1836, by Judge William Wilson and a General David White, who supposedly earned the rank of general for his heroics in the War of 1812. The local histories emphasize the "supposedly" part. When the two men were deciding what to call the little settlement in the deep woods of the Maumee Valley, White said he wanted to name it for himself: "Whiteford." My feeling: This guy must have been a bit of a bullshit artist, a creative con man—you probably had to be in those days to survive on the frontier—and I think that during my drug years, when I was lying to everyone in order to get what I needed to live, I was carrying on a proud local tradition.

Fortunately, Judge Wilson must have read the riot act to the general, and the town was eventually named the way he wanted it. Sylvania—from the Latin *silvanus*, or "forest"—is a pretty name, and appropriate. Located at the junction of two creeks, Ten Mile Creek (which—I love this—is actually thirty miles long) and Ottawa Creek, the land was heavily forested, mostly with hardwoods such as oak, walnut, elm, and ash. "The forests of the early times were dense and dangerous," wrote one local historian. "Possibly this is one of the reasons Sylvania was located at the junction of the two creeks."

There were Indians here; the Indian wars of early America, in fact, were fought out all along the Maumee River Valley. Massacres and countermassacres, for almost half a century. The woods around Sylvania were rich in game, which attracted roving bands of Huron and Chippewa. Two of their camping grounds were later the site of local golf courses—another reminder of who won that war.

The railroad arrived in Sylvania a year or so after its founding, and with it came industry. Soon there were sawmills, a tannery, a barrel stave factory, grist mills, livery stables, and other small industries serving the town. In the years prior to the Civil War, Sylvania became a stop on the Underground Railroad, ferrying escaped slaves from the South to Canada. Not surprisingly, Sylvania was staunchly pro-Union when the Civil War broke out. A total of 102 men from the town served in the Union army; 26—1 out of 4 who served—were killed. This is Sylvania: a hardworking, flag-waving town, with a few secrets.

In 1961 Sylvania was officially given city status. Although

the chamber of commerce brochures now claim a population of 46,000, the "city" center itself is about 17,500. And it still feels more like a town to me than a city. If you can judge by the number of churches—thirty—it's a devout community. And if you count the number of schools—two senior and three junior high schools, seven elementary schools, five private schools, and Lourdes College, a four-year private liberal arts college—you'd have to surmise that it's a city that cares about education. Above all, Sylvania—like so many similar Midwest communities—takes pride in being a family place. "A great place to live and raise a family," says the chamber of commerce. "The school system, parks, recreation, heritage, museum, bike paths and fine neighborhoods, all make it a balanced community."

When I hear that stuff I'm tempted to say that there is a chemical imbalance beneath it all. The truth is Sylvania really does lives up to much of what the town boosters make it out to be. The taxes are low, the cost of living moderate, the services good. These days we're mostly a bedroom community for Toledo—where many residents commute, to work for Dana, Libbey Glass, Jeep, all of which have headquarters there—so in many ways we are a prototypical American suburb. It is indeed a "great place" to raise a family, which is why my wife and I are doing exactly that.

Still, understanding my addiction, or anybody's addiction in this country, requires recognition that drugs and alcohol are not confined to the so-called lower classes. Sylvania is most definitely not Compton or the South Bronx. But just because the paychecks are fat and the lawns lush, just because no one's ever thought to shoot an episode of *Cops* in Sylvania, doesn't mean the place is immune to the misery of drugs and alcohol. It's here, just like it's everywhere in this country.

Thinking that *it can't happen here* not only unfairly stereotypes every inner-city person as a drug addict, but also fails to get to the roots of the problem, which are complex. Even today there are many in Sylvania who don't like to admit that this stuff went on and goes on. I hear this from some city officials and community leaders who simply deny that there is a problem. Rather, they think *I* was the problem. Their attitude is: *Todd was bad, Sylvania wasn't.* Even today, my old high school won't let me come speak, because in all my other talks, to schools all over the country, I reference the fact that I started doing drugs while I was there.

That's not to say Northview High was the reason I became an addict. However, like a lot of other schools and communities in this country, they are in serious denial. Hey, I *was* a problem. I *was* bad. Horrible, in fact. But those drugs didn't come out of a vacuum. I didn't travel to Detroit to get them (at least not at first). They were here. They are here. And like alcohol, when those get into the wrong hands, the hands of an addict, you've got trouble. No matter where you are. No matter who your parents are.

For about a year my dad and I lived together, while Louise had moved away to wrestle with her demons. I have no recollections of a sense of loss, or of wondering where my mother had gone, during this period. I do, however, remember getting clocked in the head with the removable seat of one of those Big Wheels by the kid next door, Casey Corn; and how honored I felt when I was invited by another neighborhood kid, Kyle McHugh, to swim in his family's backyard pool, quite a prestigious thing in Sylvania in those days. I also recall that there was large bush on our cul-de-sac and at one point a huge hornets' nest had been built on the top. This thing was massive, and the kids in the neighborhood set out to destroy it. I remember getting ahold of my dad's garden hose, pulling it outside on the street, and blasting the nest full of water. I'd say that this was an early sign of my destructive nature, except for the fact that an older kid outdid me. This guy shot flaming arrows at the thing, like in some medieval siege, and he succeeded in setting it ablaze. Come to think of it, I wonder where that kid ended up.

In December 1972, two years and three months after my mom committed suicide, we moved into a two-story, three-bedroom Colonial house that Dad had built for us in the then-fashionable Grove Bell neighborhood of Sylvania. The house was, and is, a warm, comfortable place, overlooking the misnamed Ten Mile Creek. When we moved in there, after Louise's death, there were woods surrounding us. I remember playing on two towering mounds of dirt while the house was being built. When we moved in, there were fields and woods all around us. Now it's all developed.

Despite having other kids around in the neighborhood and in school, I felt a sense of isolation and emptiness during much of my childhood. This was only relieved on weekends, when I got to travel cross-town to my grandmother's house. It was only a mile and a half, but to me it felt like another country. Lillian Ward Crandell, or "Granny" as I've called her since I could first talk, is a tough, strong woman, now eighty-nine years old. Granny was born in 1916, six weeks after her father died. Her mother died when she was eleven, and Lillian went to live with kindly uncles and aunts. They were poor farmers in central Ohio, reduced to eating the crops they grew as the Depression set in. Eventually Lillian married and had two sons, my uncle Bill, born in 1942, and my dad Terry, two years later.

She came from a poor but loving family; they endured a lot, as did so many people of that era, and she has been the rock of my life. Granny filled in for my mom, and supplemented the role of my stepmom, as best she could. Out on her spacious, green backyard, also overlooking Ten Mile Creek, the world seemed a very different place. I remember playing with my Tonka trucks in her basement, building an igloo on her snow-covered front lawn one winter's day, helping her collect acorns and buckeyes, and talking as she knitted. At Granny's I was (and still am) safe, understood, and always loved.

Another woman entered my life at this point. My dad had met Cindy DuVall while she was working in a local drugstore, not long after Louise died. They were married in September 1972. The fact that Terry and Cindy have now been together for thirty-three years would suggest that she was the right woman for Dad. But for me, she was a disaster. Not because of who she is, but because of who I was becoming. Cindy tried to love me like a son, but I never really allowed her to. And when my half-brother Jason came along in 1974, that sealed it. This was not my "real" family, as far as I was concerned, even at age eight.

Of course, my attitude was wrong and hurtful. And while I would use my sense of isolation from my father's "second" family as another excuse later, it was not really the case. I chose to be isolated. In fact, I allowed myself to piss everything away.

Ultimately, I'm convinced that being an addict comes down to your individual makeup. Heredity plays a role, circumstances can make it less or more likely, but bottom line: It's you, my friend, the kind of person you are and the choices that you and you alone make, that will determine which way you go.

What kind of person was I becoming? Signs of tenacity were evident early. Although I don't remember it, I have seen pictures and heard my dad describe my efforts to ride an adult-sized bicycle at age three. There I am, a little blond-haired kid in bare feet and no helmet (I would never let my four-year-old son do this today), standing up and somehow managing to push the bike essentially by jumping from one pedal to the next. This has been pointed to by my dad as evidence of the determination and strong will that would later bring me close to ruin, and then eventually save my life.

I was also becoming a force to be reckoned with among the

elementary school crowd. I organized bike races on the block, which I'd promote by distributing flyers that I'd drawn at home with crayons around the neighborhood. I won most of these races, in part because of a fierce competitiveness and refusal to lose (kind of humorous when you consider what a loser I became). I was a leader in the Grove Bell neighborhood, and often I led in the wrong direction. When we got tired of racing our bikes, for example, I would lead the kids around the neighborhood after dinner and knock over all the garbage cans set up for trash collection. At holiday time, we'd do the same things with Christmas lights—we'd ride by and kick or smash them with a baseball bat.

Even more ominous signs of my character development manifested themselves in an episode that I never told anyone, until now. In the woods near our house, one of the neighborhood children and I once found an old "fort" that some older kids had built. It was some setup: There was carpeting on the floor that had been dug into the ground, surrounded by a wall and roof made of plywood and logs. There was even a door and windows. Had I stumbled on this thing ten years later, I might have decided to move in. But at that time, at age six or seven, we decided to set it on fire. Using matches from a pack we swiped from home, we lit up some old papers we'd found inside the fort and threw them on the rug. We thought it was a cool idea, but then it got out of control, as the fire spread from the structure to nearby trees and bushes; we ended up running home with the thing in full blaze behind us. Soon we heard the sound of fire engines screaming into our neighborhood. Fortunately, the fire was put out before it could spread too far. Also, thankfully, we were never caught, by either the authorities or the teenagers who had built that elaborate shack.

Still, that little exercise in pyromania was a hint of the destructive nature that I had inside me—an instinct that I would eventually channel in another direction: right back at myself.

One day a girl in my school came up to me when I was standing around with a bunch of other kids and said, "Todd's mother jumped off a bridge and killed herself." As I'd been told the story, my mom had been killed in a car accident. I cursed her out, for lying. But inside the curiosity was growing. On Christmas Eve when I was in third grade, around 1974, we were at Granny's house. I went to use her bathroom, and noticed a letter that had accidentally been left out on the counter. I recognized my dad's handwriting. It was explaining to my grandmother what had happened that night on Route

23. To this day, I'm not sure why he needed to write this down when he could have just told her. Maybe it was too hard to verbalize. Anyway, I read his account of what happened to Louise and saw the word *suicide*. I'm not sure if I knew what it meant, but I pieced it all together: My mom had killed herself. When I put the letter down, I remember feeling a sense of satisfaction that the little bitch who taunted me in school had been wrong. My mom didn't jump off a bridge. She drove into one. And I certainly wasn't traumatized, at least initially. As I recall, finding the letter was only the second most impressive thing to me that Christmas. My life-sized Wile E. Coyote stuffed animal—which was about the same size as I was—was way more interesting.

Psychologists might say that I sublimated, or buried, the memory of that traumatic discovery that night. It would slowly gnaw its way through my soul over the next few years. Now I knew the truth about Louise and Terry Crandell. Now I knew that I was the child of a mother who had chosen to kill herself rather than live with me.

Me and my parents, circa 1968.

2

Fried on Ice

When I make presentations at schools, I usually begin by asking this question:

"How many of you want to grow up and become a drug addict?"

I always get the same reaction: furrowed brows, smirks, a few nervous giggles, and incredulous looks exchanged among the kids, as if to say, *Yeah, right. What a dumb question. What loser would make it their goal to be addicted to drugs?* The answer of course is that no one, certainly no young person, would deliberately set out to put themselves through the hell of addiction. Nobody wants to become an alcoholic or drug addict, and yet millions do, including me.

The reasons why are complex and the focus of a great deal of study and debate. One thing the experts agree on is that there seems to be some sort of genetic predisposition toward addiction. I certainly believe that's true; that I inherited the traits to become a drug addict, just as I inherited my eye color, my height, and my body's propensity for producing cholesterol. But does that fully explain what happened to me? In a way, I wish it was so. During the time I was using, that would have been a wonderful excuse. "Sorry, can't help myself," I would say, as I downed ten valiums washed down by five shots of Jack Daniels. "My genes are making me doing this. It's inherited, don't you know?"

Yes, it's true that both my mother and her brother were addicts and that I probably inherited this trait. But there are millions of other people who come from similar backgrounds and don't have a problem. Scientists now estimate that alcoholism has a heritability of only 40 to 60 percent. This is evident in the fact that even in families with alcohol or drug problems, you'll usually find at least one sibling who is *not* affected. What makes one sibling a self-destructive addict and the other a respected professional who can drink socially if he chooses? What makes one person recognize that she can't "handle" alcohol and stop or moderate it while someone else, like me, just keeps on pounding 'em down? No one knows for sure, but the latest theory is that addiction is influenced by a combination of factors—hereditary, psychosocial, and situational factors (or to put it more simply, your genes, your environment, and the situation you find yourself in). A recent study was able to get closer than ever in pinpointing this relationship: At Uppsala University in Sweden, researchers found that the presence of a specific genotype thought to cause alcoholism, *as well as* family relations, could predict alcohol consumption. It was the interaction of the two that was critical. "A hereditary risk for alcohol consumption 'amplifies' the risk from a poor environment and/or vice-versa," said Dr. Kent W. Nilsson, one of the researchers. "Furthermore, our results suggest that a hereditary risk may be prevented if the environment is good."

Clearly, there's more to it than "just" your genes. There are circumstances that arise and there are choices we make that will increase or decrease the likelihood of us "realizing" our genetic potential. Based on this study, I had two strikes against me: hereditary and a poor family environment. But I also made bad choices, including the choice not to help make the family environment better, by perhaps being a little more receptive to my stepmom and half brother and not always causing problems. Later, my decision-making abilities would improve; otherwise I wouldn't be writing this today. But early on, the poor judgment I showed . . . my inability to deal with the genetic hand I had been dealt, as well as the turbulent family situation I found myself in . . . ruined the thing most precious to me.

Hockey.

You see, like the kids I talk to today, I didn't want to grow up to become an addict, either. What I wanted to do was play in the NHL.

I know most people think that ice hockey is popular only in Canada and maybe in a few cold-weather U.S. locales, such as Minnesota or Massachusetts. But there has long been a robust hockey scene here in the heartland. Here in Ohio and neighboring Michigan, there are outstanding youth and junior teams and some very good high school and college teams. A number of professional players also hail from the Buckeye State. Sylvania happens to be one of those communities where hockey was popular—popular enough that I didn't have to go searching for the game. It found me.

My dad, his new wife, Cindy, and I moved into our new home in the Grove Bell neighborhood in December 1972. There was a frog pond near the house and old Ten Mile

Creek running behind it. Back then, both would freeze for much of the winter. Shortly after we arrived, in the early months of 1973, I started watching the neighborhood kids playing hockey on the pond. I was six years old. I remember telling my dad that I wanted to play, too. "You have to learn to skate first," he said.

I honestly can't remember the first time I ventured out on the ice to join the local kids. In my mind, it's almost as if I was suddenly there, on a pair of cheap Rally skates, gliding— awkwardly at first, I'm sure—across a shimmering surface. And once I was there, I never wanted to leave. Most of us have idyllic childhood memories; the time and place when everything seemed so perfect, we almost wish our lives could have stayed frozen in that moment. For me, those moments are frozen indeed. I'm on the ice at the frog pond by the Grove Bell house playing hockey. I'm six or seven and the harsh Midwest cold has made my cheeks red and my nose a little runny. But it doesn't bother me, because I've found this place, almost like another dimension, where I can fly across a flat shiny surface, zigzagging around other skaters, on and on through a golden sunset. And I've got a hockey stick in my hands.

I took to the game right away. The fast pace of play, the

clatter of the sticks, the twinkle of the ice slivers that would appear when skates carve the surface, with that beautiful *shruppp* sound: It was all magic to me. At age eight, I joined my first team. I was a "Mite" playing in the Sylvania youth hockey league, sponsored by Hammill Manufacturing, a local tool and die maker. I played defense that year as well as the next, in the nine-year-old league, when I played for the Rems Flyers. Even then, I had already taken a liking to the idea of trying to stop the puck. I didn't want to score, I wanted to deny those who would score on me. I liked the idea of somehow blocking—smacking down, catching, kicking away—this black, hard rubber disk that might come flying at me any moment, from any angle.

This was all leading me to one place: the net. In hockey, the guy who stands in front of it, defending against the shots of the opposing team, is the goalie. It's a position that, some say, is one of the toughest to play in all sports. One reason I was the natural choice was that no one else wanted to do it. Goalies have a reputation for being cocky, for having a kind of gun-slinger attitude. *You think you can shoot that puck past me? I say you can't. Let's get it on.* This suited me fine.

In the days before cable, I would watch the Toronto Maple Leafs play on CBC, Channel 9, which we'd pick up from

Windsor, Ontario. I became an avid fan watching the Leafs, and within a short time I was watching every NHL game we could pick up, paying close attention to the goalies. My favorite was Billy Smith of the New York Islanders. We had the same birthday, December 12, and (so I thought) the same kind of personality. Born in Perth, Ontario, in 1950, and nicknamed "Battling" Billy, Smith had a temper and wasn't afraid to use his stick on players crowding the crease, the semicircle around the goalie's nest. He played fiercely, and he never took any guff from any opposing player.

Oh yeah, and he was a winner. The Islanders of my boyhood, the 1970s, were an expansion club that was developing into a powerhouse; a team that would go on to win four straight Stanley Cups from 1980 through 1983. And Smith was one of the keys to their success. He shut out the best players of his generation including, in one memorable Stanley Cup final against the Edmonton Oilers, both Wayne Gretzky and Mark Messier, two of the greatest scorers in NHL history. He was even a lefty, like me. Boy, did I want to be Billy Smith.

I have never met Smith. But in 1973, I would meet a guy who would have a more profound and direct effect on my hockey and on my life than any NHL star: Jim Cooper, who at that time was the manager of the local indoor rink, the Tam O'Shanter in Sylvania, would coach me on several youth teams and later at Northview High School, where he became head hockey coach in 1975 and continues to this day. Tall, thin Coop spoke with a deep, resonant, and reassuring voice. He was generally cool and calm on the outside, and a warm, caring man on the inside, who became and remains one of my closest friends.

Coop had played hockey at Whitmer High School in Toledo, which would later become our big rival. He had just been hired as the rink manager in 1974 when my stepmom brought me there. He remembers me—in his words—as "a little towhead blond with one of those cereal bowl haircuts." I didn't have skate guards to protect the flimsy blades of those skates, so Coop carried me across the parking lot and onto the ice.

With the skills I was learning at the Tam, and my single-minded dedication to hockey, I became a pretty decent player; good enough that in 1975, at age nine, I began playing for the local travel team. Shriner Realty was our sponsor, and appropriately so as we covered a lot of real estate that season, traveling all over the upper Midwest playing other youth teams. I would do this, on various teams, for seven long seasons, spending almost every weekend from the end of August until mid-March on the road. We played in Detroit, Cincinnati, Columbus, Cleveland, Chicago. We traveled to Pennsylvania, New Jersey, West Virginia, and the mecca of hockey, Canada, where we played teams in Windsor, Toronto, and Montreal. Our teams were good, too—and, I'm proud to say, I think I was an important part of their success. They knew that with "TC" (as my teammates started to call me) in the net, we had a chance, so long as our guys could score a few, which they usually did.

In 1980 I was selected to play for a Toledo-based team that competed in the Michigan National League. We were the only Ohio team in that league, which produced a number of outstanding college players, and a number of future NHL stars, including Pat LaFontaine, who became a star with the Rangers and Islanders; Al Iafrate of the Toronto Maple Leafs; and Jimmy Carson of the Detroit Red Wings. It was another rung on a ladder that I felt was surely leading me to a career in professional hockey.

Seven years is a long time for a young person. Through hockey, I not only traveled the interstates of Ohio and Michigan to exotic places like Fort Wayne, Indiana, and Trenton, New Jersey, but I also took a personal journey from childhood to adolescence. The game, however, was really all that mattered to me. Not school, not the family I now felt estranged from. Those proverbial inner demons—conjured in part by the discovery of that letter revealing my mother's suicide—were dormant inside my mind, but about to come alive.

It began in May 1980, near the end of eighth grade. I was at a party at the house of a kid who was already headed for trouble. His parents were away, and he and a few of his other buddies had managed to score some cheap beer. At one point in the party, they brazenly whipped out cans, popped the tops, and started drinking. Impulsively, I asked one of the guys if I could try some. "Sure," he said, passing the can over to me. I took a sip of beer. Almost as soon as I swallowed, a sort of shimmer seemed to run down the length of my body. I remember distinctly realizing that I'd crossed some kind of line at that moment and sensing that my life was going to change, and not for the better. I was right: This was an important threshold.

Let's go back to the scientific literature for a moment. The age at which a person takes his or her first drink has been carefully studied by researchers in substance abuse (it's deemed important enough that it rates its own acronym:

AFD, age of first drink). In 2001 a University of Michigan study found that adolescents with at least one parent who experienced an early AFD were more likely to do so themselves. (I don't know exactly how old my mom was when she took her first drink, but considering that she was a heroin addict by the time she was twenty-one, it's a safe bet she was pretty young.) In addition, these "children of early AFD parents," especially the boys, were more likely to demonstrate what the researchers called "conduct disorder" and a pattern of rebelliousness.

This was me to a t. I'm almost surprised these researchers didn't find that these adolescent males from early AFD families also tended to become goalies on hockey teams.

I only had a few sips that night. I didn't get drunk or demand to have more and more. Still, in the back of mind, I knew something was wrong. Fast-forward three months. I'm now entering my freshman year at Northview High School in Sylvania. Still playing hockey on a hotshot travel league team, still living in Grove Bell, still just a kid who has taken just a few sips of beer. The Friday night after our first week of school, some buddies of mine had planned to go watch Northview's football team play their opening game of the season. We decided to have a few drinks first. Hey, we were now big-shot freshman, we'd survived the first week of school, it was the first time a lot of us had seen each other since last June . . . so what the heck. We went to my friend Gary's house. Years later, he would be the best man at my wedding, but if he had never spoken to me again after that night as freshman in 1980, I would have understood. We opened the liquor cabinet in his parent's house, I spotted a bottle of Jack Daniels, cracked it open, and began guzzling. I consumed an entire fifth of that stuff—the whole bottle—and to top it off took two hits of speed that I'd bought. By the time we got to the football game, I could hardly stand up. Gary told me later I turned blue, and he got scared that I was going to die. We couldn't go to the game with me like that, so he and the other guys—none of whom had drunk nearly as much me—had to carry me back to his house. When we got back there, I had to use the bathroom. I went into what I thought was his bathroom, and urinated all over Gary's closet, ruining a brand-new jacket.

I'd gone from taking a few sips of a beer to chugging a fifth of Jack Daniels with a speed chaser just the second time I'd indulged. I should have realized then that this was not for me. Instead, it was just the opposite.

I wanted more. The beast within me was up on its hind legs and baying.

That kind of behavior continued during my freshman and sophomore years. I wasn't drinking every day, only on weekends. But when I did, I would drink until I passed out, or couldn't remember what happened. It was beginning to affect my hockey. I'd go out drinking with my buddies on Friday night, get wasted, and the next day when we'd play a game, I felt awful. This was the progression of addiction. This was also about the time my friends started to notice that something was wrong with me. A couple of their parents even called my parents to tell them that I was having a problem. They refused to believe it. My dad's attitude was, *How could this be? He's a star athlete, he knows what his mom went through, he wouldn't touch the stuff.* Of course, I fed this illusion, swearing up and down that I wasn't drinking.

I was sixteen now, about to enter my junior year at Northview High School. My hockey career was going really well. I had played well in the Michigan National League and it was time now for me to take the next step, to the Junior A League. Despite its name, the "Juniors" are akin to a developmental league in major league baseball: the first stepping-stone to a professional career. My family had been on vacation in Cape Cod, and the day we came back the letter arrived, from Paddock Pools, one of the big sponsored Junior

A League teams in Detroit. They were inviting me to join them.

I remember running right from the mailbox into my house to tell my dad. "That's great," he said. "But you know you're not playing there." I was dumbfounded. My dad said there was no way he would allow me, a sixteen-year-old with a new license and (he already suspected) some questionable behaviors, to drive an hour from Sylvania to Detroit every day after school. It was a real blow.

He and I still disagree on this. I have four young children now, and if one of them ever has an opportunity to do something special with a talent, be it playing hockey or the violin, I'm going to get behind them and help take them as far as they want to go with it.

In retrospect, I see that moment as decisive: a detour that killed my chances for becoming a professional hockey player and helped put me on the road to becoming an addict. In fairness to my dad, Coach Cooper doesn't think it would have made a difference. "The real death of that dream came with the decision to get involved in all of this off-ice curricular crap," he said. "That would have happened whether you went to Detroit or not."

Regardless, instead of an eager young player in Juniors, I

was now an angry, dispirited kid on my way to playing for Coop on a Northview High School team that was inferior to the one I could have joined in Detroit. I could have tried to be a more constructive member of the Northview team; I could have kept my act together. Instead, I joined the high school that fall thinking, *You're lucky to have me . . . and I'm going to play my way.* So I flouted rules, often angered Coach Cooper, but played well enough that I could get away with it.

I had a good year in goal as a junior at Northview. Not only had I fine-tuned my game, I'd fine-tuned my arrogant attitude. I liked to make big flashy saves, giving the shooters on the other team more of a target by positioning myself at an angle that would reveal a little of the net behind me. It was a tease. When they'd try to put it through, I'd shoot my glove up there and stop it. I played what the goalies called "butter-fly" style (Smith did this, too). When the other team was around my net, I'd get down on both knees with my legs out to the side in a V-position. I'd provoke fights, too, egging the opposition on so they'd lose their cool. When one of the opposing players would finally get so ticked off he'd throw a punch, I had my big goons on the team who'd come out and beat the stuffing out of that guy, who in turn would also get a penalty for having started the melee.

It got so that not only other teams but also their fans got to know me. In the game before the state finals that year, we played our archrival, Whitmer High School in Toledo. They were a good team; some of their guys had played with me in the Michigan National League. The Whitmer fans hated my guts because of my showboat attitude. That night a whole bunch of them crowded around the glass behind the net, screaming "Crandell sucks!" I loved it. The game was really close. At one point, Whitmer got a penalty shot. That's a one-on-one situation: The puck is placed on center ice, and the player on offense gets to take the puck to the net with only the goalie of the penalized team there to defend against him. Stopping one of these is tough yet critical; a successful penalty shot can change the momentum of a game. That night, the Whitmer player—a good skater and shooter, one of my former teammates from the National League—skated toward me, took his shot, and I made a fancy glove stop to deny him. Immediately I bolted out of the net, skated right up to the glass where all those Crandell-hating fans were congregated, and gave 'em the finger. Boy did that tick them off.

We lost that game, 2-1, because our defense fell apart with 1:17 left. I was angry, of course, but I must say I got a certain satisfaction out of the fact that the Whitmer security guards had to escort me out of the building for my own safety.

While my game was coming together, the rest of my life was falling apart. I was now drinking every day. And I had moved beyond hits of speed to other drugs: marijuana, Valium. It still wasn't bad as it would become, but it was getting there. By my senior year, I was packing my bong along with my goalie mask and pads when I went off to practice every morning at five fifteen. At six thirty or seven, as soon as I got out of a practice, I'd head back to my car with some buddies of mine, and we would fire up that bad boy, inhaling a dime bag or so of weed before classes started. This would continue throughout the day: weed, valiums, tranquilizers, alcohol. In the parking lot, in the boys' room, sometimes even in the classroom, when we had a substitute teacher.

How does a junior in high school get the money to have a car and buy all these drugs? Well, I worked part-time at the family business, Sylvan Studios, manufacturers of awards ribbons and plaques, where I put medals together, doing mailings and other menial stuff. That helped pay for the booze and the weed. Valium, speed, and any other type of pharmaceutical was at my disposal thanks to a friend who worked at a drugstore and did me favors.

Somehow I managed to get passing grades, but if I could have, I would have just played hockey and partied. By my senior year, my hair was getting long, I had gotten my left ear pierced, and I walked around all the time wearing sunglasses. I wanted to look like a heavy-metal goalie—a member of Mötley Crüe on skates. Coop wasn't happy. He would give me lectures about cleaning up my act, and I would "yes" him to death, then go back to what I was doing.

My senior year began on an inauspicious note. The first Friday of school, I did my first line of coke. I instantly knew I had found what I was looking for in the drug world. That stuff grabbed ahold of me and wouldn't let go—nor did I want it to. I was amped up out of control, and coke soon became a daily part of my life. I did a few lines before school, before practice, before everything. I was joined in this new passion by my friend Ferd, a terrific hockey player I knew from the Michigan League who had just transferred to Northview. Hockey, cocaine, and my buddy Ferd: A winning combination as far as I was concerned. And it seemed that way, when the season began.

In retrospect, I don't know how I even got out on the ice, as wasted as I was. But we did, and we played pretty well. Early that season we beat my former travel team from Toledo, 2-1.

I had a good game, and was really stoked about that.

In November 1984, the night before we were leaving for a major state tournament at Miami University in Oxford, I got busted for underage drinking by the cops. A few of us were driving around Sylvania. We stopped at a traffic light and my buddy Ferd, who was driving, lit up a joint. Bad timing. There was a cop right next to us. Ferd tried to pretend it was a cigarette he was smoking, holding it nonchalantly between his two fingers. The cop didn't fall for it; he pulled us over, finding the weed in the front seat and my case of beer in the back. They took us to the local jail. We didn't get charged, however, and were released to the custody of our parents—who, of course, weren't very pleased. Somehow, Coop got word of what happened. I went with the team to Miami, but when we got there he made me sit out a game. Still, he didn't tell the school because he knew what the penalty would have been.

Ferd made a big difference on the team, and he helped raise my game as well. We won the first three games after the Christmas break. Ferd had twenty-seven points in those games, and I had two shutouts. The third game in that streak was memorable, for a number of reasons. It started with Ferd and I buying a quarter ounce of coke, which is a lot of blow, for four hundred dollars, which was a lot of money for two high school kids. We were playing a team from Jackson, Michigan, and for the entire ninety-mile ride to the game we did lines in the back of the bus.

This was a big game for a number of reasons. First, we were on a roll; a victory here was one more step toward the state championships. Second, Sylvania Northview had a history of bad blood with Jackson Lumen Christie High School and their fans were as rowdy and vocal as Whitmer's. Before the game started, Coop told me to make sure I didn't skate off the ice with the other team at the end of the second period. So what did I do? The horn blows after the second period, we're already kicking their butts, their team's coming off the ice, and instead of waiting and skating off with the Northview guys into our locker room as I was ordered to do, I skate right through the team from Michigan. In hockey, that's a flagrant violation of etiquette, especially with two teams who don't like each other to begin with. Words were exchanged, and in a few seconds, fists were flying. It started a big melee.

In the locker room Coop was furious, and rightly so. He grabbed my face mask and shook it: "I told you not to do that!" he screamed. I just shrugged, and sniffed. Apparently, I had been doing that a lot. "What's the matter?" he said, puzzled. "You have a cold?"

Despite the drugs and the fight, that night was one of the best of my career. I stopped sixty shots, Ferd and the rest of the guys were awesome, and we won 10-0, my second shutout in three games. On the bus ride home that night, we celebrated with more coke, snorting our lines in the back where we thought none of the adults could see us.

The next morning, Coop called. Even now, twenty years later, he remembers it as "one of the most tragic days of my life." On the phone, his voice was trembling. I thought at first somebody had died. "How could you do this to me?" he said. I didn't know what he was talking about. He told me that someone on the team had reported to him that we were doing drugs on the bus. I denied it, forgot about the whole thing, and went to school on Monday as if nothing had happened. After class, I ambled into the locker room for practice, as usual. I was half dressed when a grim-looking Coop came in and told me he wanted to talk to me in his office. I went in; he closed the door and told me I was out: kicked off the team. The words were barely out of his mouth when I ran out of his office, half dressed in pads and skates, dove across the locker room bench where a bunch of my teammates were getting dressed, and tried to strangle the guy whom I knew had ratted us out.

I didn't think so at the time, but Coop did what he had to do. "I had an obligation to the parents of the other kids on the team to protect their kids from that stuff," he says today. "I had to remove you and Ferd for the good of the group."

Maybe so, but even Coop had no control over what would happen next. That night, the school principal apparently held a little inquest into this situation. Parents and kids were called in to "testify." No one called me or my parents, however, until the next morning. During second period, I was handed a note directing me to the principal's office immediately. When I arrived, Ferd was walking out. "Just resign or we'll be in more trouble," he whispered loudly as I entered the office of the principal, who sat there with his sternest *you're in real trouble, young man* mien.

The athletic director was seated to his right. Both of these men were new in their jobs, a fact that I either didn't know or couldn't appreciate at the time. The principal started talking, and his demeanor was dead-on: I was in real trouble. He accused me of using drugs on the team bus. I acted like James Cagney under the hot lights. "You don't have anything on me," I said, like the insolent wise guy I was.

Then the athletic director, whom I had taken a strong dislike to during his first few months at Northview, started talking. I glared at him. This guy, I thought in my anger, didn't know anything about the situation, and now he was butting in. Where was my coach? Where was my accuser? Where was anybody who had actually been there?

Later Coop would learn that he was under suspicion as well; that there concerns that he was too loose in his program and couldn't "control" the kids on the team. Pure baloney, of course—he was and is a great asset to that school and to our community. Still, the decision that had been arrived at, without his input, was draconian.

Then I heard the principal say the words. "We're expelling you. If you don't agree and sign this, we're going to turn this over to the police." Again, I snapped. This time I lunged across the desk trying to get the AD. People rushed in to break it up. It was like another hockey melee, except this time there was no way to make a save. I was out. My hockey career was over. I'd been kicked out of school. A whole new nightmare world beckoned.

In the early years of travel hockey.

3

Fear and Loathing in Cocoa Beach

The next morning I was lying in bed with no hockey team to play for, no school to go to, and a growing sense of nothing to live for.

I heard the phone ring. A few minutes later, the door to my room flew open. It was my dad standing there, hands on hips, with a disgusted look on his face. He had just learned what happened. "This is the worst day of my life since your mother killed herself," he said. Well, there it was, out in the open at last. We argued—I tried to tell him that I hadn't done anything (a lie), and that the school principal and AD had no proof (the truth). He didn't want to hear it and stormed out. My brother Jason, then about ten, asked my stepmom what was going on. She made a point of saying, loud enough for me to hear, "Your brother's a drug addict."

Good morning.

For a couple of days I was in shock over what had happened to me at Northview—my hockey career over in an instant, along with my high school education—and I wasn't the only one. "I was stunned," Coach Cooper says. Looking back on it today, he says, "I wanted you punished, but not kicked off the boat without a life jacket." Of the school administrators who made the decision (without Coop's input), he says, "I've come to know these men, and respect them, but at that moment I definitely felt they overreacted."

As far as my dad was concerned, I had screwed up for the last time. Our little tête-à-tête that morning ended with me being kicked out of the house. I crashed at the house of my girlfriend at the time while I tried to get back into high school. First I applied to Whitmer, our hockey rival. The response to by their administration was pretty much the same as their boisterous fans: "Crandell sucks." They didn't want any part of me. Neither did any of the other area schools I applied to. So there I was: an eighteen-year-old drug addict with no home to go to, no school to go to—and, within a few days, no job to go to, either. Anderson's, a big home and garden store, fired me from my menial job.

As is common with people who walk around in a drug-induced haze, there are unexpected moments of startling clarity. I had one of those a few weeks after being expelled. I realized that I didn't want to end up pumping gas or delivering pizzas for the rest of my life. I decided I was going to have to lose face, bow down, and make nice to whomever had I to in order to get back into Northview, starting with my dad. They weren't going to let me back in if I listed my address as Sylvania Park. Dad agreed to allow me to return home, provided that I remain sober. I responded with the drug addict mantra: "Sure, sure . . . yeah, yeah . . . I promise."

I had no intention, of course, of fulfilling that part of the bargain. But I was determined to get back to Northview. First we tried the aggressive approach: I showed up with our attorney one night at a school board meeting. They wouldn't even let us speak. But that summer, for reasons unexplained, they changed their mind. I was told I could re-enroll at Northview in September, to finish the last few credits I needed to earn my diploma. I was glad for the opportunity, but coming back was a humbling, humiliating experience. In the halls, in the classrooms, in the cafeteria, I'd hear the whispers and mutters. "It's Crandell . . . kicked off the team . . . can't play hockey anymore

... screwed up big-time ... still doing drugs ..." All of it true. I had been a big shot just a few months earlier, but my original class had now graduated and moved on to college, the service, or full-time jobs; and I was still sitting in algebra class, like some idiot who had been left back.

It was a lonely time. Most of the other kids had been warned about me and told to stay away. But one girl saw something beyond the teenage pariah I had become. Her name was Kathleen, a blond, straitlaced, all-American girl from the heartland. She sensed that there was more to me than the drugs, the booze, the *bad-news-loser* reputation that I was deservedly tagged with. We started dating, she a junior cheerleader, me a fifth-year cocaine-addicted senior. For a little while, Kathleen actually got me to stop doing blow— quite an achievement, considering that I was at the time doing about a gram a day (most of it before or after school— I wasn't going to take the risk of having someone rat me out again).

She told me she didn't care what happened in my past; she liked me for who I was. That was hard for me to accept— after all, even *I* didn't like who I was—and she saw through my feeble attempts to live up to her "good guy" expectations. When she heard I was back drinking and doing coke, that was it. She broke up with me. That night, I got really loaded. I hated myself so much and I couldn't even figure out why: Was it because I had screwed up the first real relationship I had ever had . . . or because I was becoming a complete slave to my addiction? Guess it didn't matter why I was trying to destroy myself . . . the important thing was that I succeeded.

To that end, I spent the following summer getting completely lost in my addiction. I had earned my high school diploma . . . not a GED, but a diploma from Northview. I took some pride in that: I had gone back and faced the music, eaten a lot of crow, but gone on to do something right for a change. I could and should have used that modest achievement to propel my life in a different trajectory. Instead, I applied my drive and commitment in other directions, such as seeing how many days in a row I could drink at least one six-pack of beer.

I kept track of this, believe it or not, on a calendar. For every day I drank six or more, I'd mark the date with a little red dot. Soon the calendar was filled with red dots. I was delighted.

It was also around this time that I got the idea in my head that I wanted to go to Florida. Somehow I felt that if I could leave Sylvania and visit my maternal grandmother in

Bradenton, she'd help me figure out how and why my life had gone wrong. I talked about this a lot, every time I got really drunk. One night, I was out partying with a friend in Bowling Green. After several hours of drinking, I actually decided to try to make the road trip. Last thing I remember was lying in a water bed with a girl named Lisa, who was writing her name in orange marker on my chest, and I was telling her about how I was determined to go to Florida. The next thing I knew I was on the floor of a cheap hotel room. No water bed, no Lisa, no orange marker; nothing but a sick, nauseous feeling and a sense of dread as to just where the hell I had ended up. I picked up the phone and a woman with a southern accent answered. "Where am I?" I asked, groggily. "You're in Perry, Georgia," she replied politely.

It was two days later. How I got from Ohio to Georgia, what I did on the way, I still don't know. I was almost out of money at that point, so I had to head back home. It was shameful: I couldn't even run away successfully. I arrived back in Sylvania early the next morning, and walked up the stairs just as my dad was heading to work. He looked at me, said "you're nothing but a drunk," shook his head, and walked past.

I didn't say a word because I knew it was the truth.

I was a drunk, an alcoholic, an addict. At what point does that happen? When do you "become" addicted to drugs or alcohol . . . or anything else, for that matter? It's hard to say, in part because addiction is a difficult concept to pin down. People are often accused of being "addicted" to shopping, cell phone use, ice cream, *Survivor*, you name it. "Is Tom Cruise a relationship addict?" was the headline in a recent online news item about the movie star's many loves.

Are these really addictions, in the same way as alcohol or drugs? Yes, according to some definitions of addiction. *Webster's,* for example, defines it as "to give oneself up to a strong habit." If that's addiction, well then my wife Melissa is addicted to *General Hospital;* and my coauthor—a New Yorker with a strong penchant for the same breakfast every morning—is addicted to bagels. And maybe Tom Cruise *is* addicted to relationships.

A better definition, I think, is this one, from a dictionary of psychological terms: "Addiction is an uncontrollable compulsion to repeat a behavior regardless of its consequences."

That "consequences" part is a key to what psychologists believe determines addiction. Provided it isn't affecting your life or health in an adverse way, watching a lot of TV, shopping, or enjoying a certain kind of food on a daily basis is not an "addiction." *No harm, no foul* seems to be the current thinking. Given that I was doing a lot of harm to myself and others around me, as a result of my uncontrollable compulsion to drink and use drugs, you could say I was a full-blown addict by this time of my life, age eighteen.

The *full-blown* concept raises another question: Are there degrees of addiction? Yes, say the experts. In fact, there's an Addiction Severity Index, a sort of addict rating system involving an in-depth interview with the subject, that delves into the family situation, frequency of use, work and arrest record . . . myriad factors. Underlying this, of course, are dozens of theories as to why addiction occurs in the first place: the disease model (addiction is an illness), the moral model (addiction is a character flaw), the genetic model (addiction is part of your hereditary makeup), the cultural model (addiction is the result of cultural influences).

As discussed earlier, all of these views have their proponents, and each makes sense to a degree. In my mind, however, none can fully explain addiction—at least my addiction or those of the people I now work with regularly. In most addicts each of the four most common causal factors is in play to a greater or lesser extent.

They also, in my opinion, allow addicts like me to do

something we learn to be very good at: finding someone or something to blame for our problems. My addiction is my mother's fault because I inherited the "bad" genes from her; my addiction is my father's fault because he remarried and didn't give me the love, support, and attention I needed; my addiction is my principal's fault, because he kicked me out of school, sending me into a downward spiral; my addiction is Mötley Crüe's fault, because I was a big fan of the band, and I heard they all liked to party.

Nonsense.

Sure, some of those factors might have played a role. Ultimately, though, it came down to me making bad choices and doing the wrong things. Later on, when I started making a few good decisions, things began to change. But not yet. Indeed, at this point in my life, I was about to make some colossally bad decisions.

First, my halfhearted attempt to go to college had ended when I quit the University of Toledo after a few weeks of classes in which I was too wasted to remember anything that any of my professors said. Then, in October, I had the big fight with my parents, in which I threw my dad into the closet and my hockey trophies got smashed. I got the boot after that, again.

In December 1986, with the Midwest winter winds starting to whip up, I blew out of Sylvania. I needed to get away
from a town where the cops knew me, the parents hated me,
and the kids either lionized me for the wrong reasons or
laughed at me behind my back, for being a stumblebum
drunk. Out of several forays to the Sunshine State, this would
be my quintessential Florida road trip, like something out of
a Hunter Thompson book. Four of us got into my 1984
Buick Regal and headed once again down Route 75 south.
One of my buddies, Chip, had just won $150,000 in an
insurance settlement, so we had money to burn. We took with
us close to half an ounce of coke (street value, about twenty-
five hundred dollars, a fifth of Bombay gin, a case of beer, and
probably a couple of ounces of weed. With the windows of
my Buick tinted—for precisely this reason—we could freely
dip into our stash.

It's funny how quickly the original purpose of my trip—
to see my grandmother—was forgotten. The first night
we arrived, we went in to a pool hall in Cocoa Beach. I met
a fifteen-year-old local named Dawnetta. After just fifteen
minutes, she was performing oral sex on me in the parking
lot. Another guy, a Trinidadian named Derrick, told us where
to find drugs. We did. Soon we were all over the place, some

nights sleeping in my car, other nights in hotels paid for by our buddy with the insurance money.

There were women, lots of women, in Florida. Especially there was Shari, a beautiful, big-hair blonde from Canada on holiday with her parents. Like Kathleen, she saw something beyond the scruffy, dirty, drunken bum she met on the beach. We hung out a lot, and I began to sense that this was really someone I could care about; I sensed she felt the same way, even though at the end of each day she'd go back to the hotel with her parents and I'd go back to my suite in the Buick Regal. The next morning, there she'd be, knocking on the passenger-seat window to wake me up.

Looking back, it's still amazing that she would want to spend so much time with someone like me. Heck, her parents even invited me to join them for dinner one evening. We talked about Canada, about hockey, had a great time, and enjoyed the meal and one another's company. I had made a point not to get too hammered that day, and it dawned on me at the end of the night that these people actually liked me, not the drunken fool that I had become.

The night after Shari and her parents left Cocoa Beach, I was depressed and headed out to the beach alone. But a good thing happened that put me right again: A guy we had met came by and told us that we could move into his condo. Who the hell knows why? Maybe he thought it was cool to have a couple of derelicts from Ohio in his pad. I immediately headed back to the Regal, found my buddy Bob, got our stuff together, and moved in. When this guy saw all the cases of booze we brought in, and the Mötley Crüe posters we immediately hung up on the wall, I bet he had second thoughts; he probably thought the Toledo chapter of the Hell's Angels had set up residence in his condo. Too late, pal. We were ready to party. Later that same day, we went back to the beach to start drinking and another good thing happened.

A really hot-looking girl, with long black hair and a pink bikini, came over to me. "Hey, would you like to party with me tonight?" she said. I looked over my shoulder as if to say *are you really talking to me?*—but she was. Her name was Katrina and she was on spring break from Georgetown University. She came to the new house later that night; I opened the door to find her standing there wearing a long, black, low-cut dress and high heels. I had on only a pair of unbuttoned jeans. She didn't care. "Let's go out to dinner," she said. "I'm buying." After an awesome dinner, we went back to the house and she asked if I'd like some cocaine and champagne. I thought I was dreaming. But there it was: She had a bag full of coke and a cold bottle of the bubbly that she had stuck in my refrigerator before we left. Katrina did a few lines with me but mainly just watched as I snorted and drank away. As we were getting buzzed, she asked if she could put some make-up on me. Make-up? *Okayyy,* I thought to myself, *this is weird, but what the hell, she paid for all this stuff, so whatever.* She began putting eyeliner on me and painting my fingernails as I continued to snort lines and suck up the champagne. Finally, after I was all made up like some South Beach transvestite, she said, "Let's go back to the beach." We walked along the shore, and as soon as we were in a secluded spot, she turned to me and demanded that I make love to her at that moment. *Gee,* I thought, *won't my makeup get smeared?* Actually, I didn't think about much at all. We had sex, she left, and I woke up the next morning on the couch, with my friends howling in laughter at my eyeliner. "What are you, auditioning for KISS?" one of them said.

I never saw or heard from Katrina again and I've always wondered just what that was all about: Some lesbian fantasy? Or maybe she was just a frustrated makeup artist? Either way, I didn't care, until I realized that it had taken me exactly twenty-four hours to break my pledge to Shari that I would not see another woman until she visited me in Ohio, which we had planned for that fall. I felt like a crumb, and responded to that emotion the best way I knew how: *Let's get loaded.*

Back on Cocoa Beach, I was sitting watching the waves when a powerfully built African American woman came up to me. She was huge—about six foot four, and a muscular two hundred pounds. She claimed to be a wrestler, and wanted to know if I wanted to go find some coke with her. "I'm there," I said. We managed to score, went back to our condo and started smoking crack out of a Budweiser can. We're getting really stoned, and suddenly who should appear but Dawnetta, the girl I'd met on my first night in Florida. She'd tracked us down and was back for more fun. Soon the wrestler and I were all cracked up; and she and Dawnetta got into a debate over who could give better oral sex. They asked me to be the judge, which of course I was delighted to do, sucking on my beer-can crack pipe as they proved their prowess.

I relate these stories today not to brag about sexual conquests, but rather to underscore just how messed up I was. This was meaningless, mindless sex. As with everything else in my life at that point, it was also done in a way that would maximize my risk. The AIDS epidemic was already running rampant, and yet I never used protection. Sex was just one more way to fill the void . . . consequences be damned.

Not all the interesting people I met in Florida were women. One day we were hanging around in a hotel room on Cocoa Beach when a guy called "Nail" showed up and asked if we wanted any drugs. He said he had earned his nickname not because he was tough or a carpenter, but because he could shove a full-sized nail up his nose and you would not be able to see it. Why not? Because "Nail" had no nasal cavity, the result of snorting a lot of drugs—and probably being smacked in the face by an iron pipe.

It's not surprising, consider Nail's drug of choice: Methamphetamine, also known as crystal or crank, is a powerful and dangerous stimulant that's more popular today than it was in the 1980s. So when Nail doled out a couple of lines of it on the table in our hotel room, we were intrigued—this was something different.

I did two lines of Nail's meth, about the length of my finger, and within five minutes I'd lost my mind. I became enraged and destructive. I smashed two windows in the hotel room, threw the TV out of one of them, ripped the shower curtain rod out of the wall, and nearly broke the bed in half by jumping up and down on it. I ended up staying awake for two days from the stuff, despite attempts to drink myself into unconsciousness.

Despite this meth-induced excitement, Cocoa Beach was getting old. Time to move on. Over the next few months, we traveled around the state of Florida. Orlando, Miami, St. Petersburg, Fort Myers, Jacksonville. It was like an old movie—where you see a montage of signposts as our hero makes his way on some great journey. Except, if this was to depict my life accurately, you'd have to show me puking over one sign, passed out by another, and urinating on a third.

In Boca Raton I did my "Scarface" thing. Through a cousin of Chip, we met up with some big-time narcos at a bar and went back to their mansion. There were guns there, bodyguards, and a ton of cocaine, which we were invited to partake of. I didn't have to be asked twice. The lines on the pool table were two fingers thick and as long as my leg. I tried to do an entire line in one huff. Soon my chest was pounding so fast from all the coke I'd ingested, I thought I was going to have a heart attack. The smartly dressed dealers watched me, laughed, and made comments to each other, some of them in Spanish. I noticed that most of them weren't even doing any coke. Looking back, it's a miracle they didn't take out a chainsaw, cut me into pieces, and throw me into the ocean, for snorting up so much of the merchandise. On the other hand, maybe they were amused by seeing somebody who so obviously enjoyed their product. Besides, you couldn't do all the coke they had in that house. Believe me, I tried.

Anyway, I woke up the next day miles away, on Miami Beach—along the part of the strip with the faded art-deco hotels, amid the homeless men. I almost felt like one of them now.

A couple of nights later, we had moved on and were sleeping in my car when we were awoken by a pounding on the windshield. A very scary-looking guy was outside, screaming incoherently. He had a Schlitz Malt Liquor Bull tattooed on his shoulder, and he was missing a few teeth. Maybe he wanted drugs or money, or maybe just a place to sleep, but I told my buddy Bob to lock the car doors, quick. The lunatic outside was threatening to smash the passenger-side door; we kept telling him we didn't have any drugs. Eventually he staggered off. It scared the hell out of me.

Not long after that, I was in a parking lot in St. Petersburg, Florida. I had been drinking all night and I was facedown on the pavement. In my stupor, I felt a tap on the back of my head. I thought it was one of my buddies fooling around. I rolled over to find myself looking up at a cop, brandishing a nightstick. "If you can't stand up, you're going to jail," he said. I clawed at the side of my car to pull myself up, and somehow managed to stand erect. He glared at me and walked away.

It was now June. I had been in Florida for six wasted months. Six more, I realized, and I'd probably be dead. From now on, I was going to get loaded in the safety of Sylvania. The next day, we headed back.

Wasted and spiraling downward.

4

A Day in the Life of the Addict

A day in my life as an addict started with regrets. Not over what I had done the previous night—often, I didn't remember, or only heard about it later from friends who were there—but regret over the simple fact that I was still alive.

Do you have any idea what a black, empty, desperate feeling that is? To wake up and say to yourself, *Damn, I didn't succeed in killing myself last night; how much stuff do I have to take?* If you're an addict, you probably know exactly what I'm talking about. If not, well . . . be glad you don't.

At that point, as my room blurred into focus, I would look to see if there was a drink next to me, maybe half a glass of vodka from the night before, so that I could have a little eye-opener. I'd also see if there was a girl sharing my bed—quite often, and I don't say this to brag, there was. Needless to say, she wouldn't be the kind you wanted to bring home to your parents, which is one reason that by age nineteen, I was out of my parents' house.

From June 1987 to March 1991, I lived in a one-room apartment in my hometown. It was located on the top floor of the building my father owned, and in which he operated his business. Yes, this is the same father who had kicked me out of the house; yet he still felt guilty enough to allow his deadbeat son to live rent-free in a flat that was transformed into the twentieth-century Midwest equivalent of a Shanghai opium den. It was a one-bedroom apartment, adequate for my needs—and my needs at that point were to basically get as messed up as I could as often as I could—and in a wonderful twist of irony, it looked out over the local police station. They made a few visits to this apartment, but if they knew everything that had been going on there under their noses, they would have shut me down faster than a crack house next to an elementary school.

I'd been caught up in the throes of addiction while living in my parents' house as a high school student—and I would then move the madness to a new location in Florida (where

I'd already spent one miserable Christmas) and finally spent a one-year, coked-up culmination of my life as an addict at my grandmother's house leading up to my sobriety. But for that four-and-a-half-year period between the ages of twenty-one and twenty-four, this little dump in downtown Sylvania was my base of operations for the ongoing quest to kill myself, a process that unfolded slowly, day by day, and came close to fruition.

Now it was time for my morning puke. If there was some blood in it, that probably meant I'd had a particularly good night—or maybe that I'd been punched by somebody, maybe even a friend, when we wrestled over the last line of coke or something. Sometimes I'd walk into the bathroom to find out that somebody else had already beat me to it—vomit on my bathroom floor or in my sink from the night before, maybe mine, maybe not. How's that for a nice way to start the day?

Occasionally it was even worse. One time I woke up covered in blood. The night before (I later learned) I had punched out a glass window and severely cut my hand and arm. I was already too wasted to do anything about it, so I'd just had another ten drinks or so, and passed out until morning. It was my boss who discovered me. I was working at that time for an ice delivery place. Because (yet again) I had not showed up for work that morning, he came to the apartment, and found a trail of blood leading from the building entrance all the way down the hall into my bedroom. He kicked open the door, where he found a blood-soaked bed and a body lying there with a sheet over its head. That would be me. He thought I was dead, but unfortunately I wasn't. Once he'd roused me and helped me clean off, how did I thank him? By asking him for the day off, of course. This had little to do with resting and healing my damaged arm; I wanted to stay home from work so that I could just lie around my apartment and get trashed all over again. My ploy didn't work that day: He dragged my butt—and bandaged-up arm—to work, and I had to drive around with him all day, feeling like crud and listening to him lecture me about how screwed up my life was.

Most of the time, I was unemployed so it didn't matter when I woke up. After the puke, I'd clean myself up. Food wasn't a high priority. If I had been really drunk, I was usually too hung over to eat; if I had been all coked up, I was usually too wired to stomach a morsel. Anyway, the refrigerator was almost empty of everything except liquids, mostly beer. (This is something that must have affected me; nowadays, I always want a full fridge. I guess it's one way of reminding myself how far I've come from a life that was empty and barren and cold as my old Frigidaire.)

So the order of the day was basically:

—Wake up.

—Puke.

—Clean up self and apartment.

—Get on the phone to try and score stuff to start the party all over again.

With the booze, it was easier, of course. The hardest part was driving myself to the liquor store, because my head would be pounding from the night before. Many times I would scribble down a note and hand it to my main man, Larry, and have him take it over to the local carry-out. They knew me there; I was what you'd call a high-volume customer. Because this was always first priority, all my money from work and dealing went toward drugs and alcohol, and I had good credit with both the carry-out and Clips, our local liquor store. So I'd write down my shopping list: two cases beer; five to ten bottles of wine; fifths of rum, vodka, Jack Daniels and Jim Beam. Larry the delivery boy would bring it back. I'd give him a little something—usually a "thanks" and an invitation to share a drink—and then, *let's party.*

Sometimes I'd run up a load of debt on my credit cards. I can remember around Christmas one year going to a liquor store and buying five hundred or six hundred dollars of booze and watching them bring it out on dollies and noticing the clerks' faces. They were looking at all this stuff and looking at me and then looking at each other as if to say, *Damn, this is a lot of booze. This guy was must be a serious party animal.* I kind of liked that. It was a way of reasserting the fact that I was the leading drunk in Sylvania. Numero uno, baby. It's a personality trait I still have. I always want to be the best at what I'm doing. At the time I wanted to be the best loser around, and I was obviously doing a pretty damn good job of it.

While I was waiting for my friends to show up with the booze or maybe some drugs they'd scored, I'd usually pull out a bottle of Southern Comfort, my preferred morning drink. I had to have something in the morning, otherwise I couldn't function. If I was working, this was happening at 7 A.M. If not, it was about 11. Either way, I'd be looking forward to my afternoon drink. After noon, I switched to rum and Coke or Jack Daniels and coke. I'd always make sure it was Diet Coke— I didn't want the extra calories. Nice, huh? I was barely twenty-one and already working on a good case of cirrhosis of the liver and stomach ulcerations, but hey, I was counting those calories. Same thing with vodka: If I was having that, I'd mix it with o.j., to make sure I was getting my vitamin C. Lot of good that was going to do me, while I was burning my guts out and frying my brain on a daily basis.

It's interesting, though: As much of a total degenerate as I was, I had been an athlete in high school, and I still tried to keep myself looking like one. As with everything else in my life, it was a mirage, a cover-up. I kept myself clean (until later at night, when I was out of my mind), always wore stylish clothes, got my hair cut, and used to lift weights regularly, so that I'd still look good for the girlies. There were even periods, usually after some really bad experience, when I'd tone down the drug and drink: Eat right, work out regularly, swear to everyone around me that I was cleaning up my act. Never lasted more than a couple of days.

If I wasn't working, I was usually pretty messed up again by noon. If not, it would just take a little longer—say, until 4 or 5 P.M. when I got off. Either way, before the sun was down I'd have downed a fifth of booze or close to it and have some drugs in me as well. If I could, I'd stay home. I knew that once I really get rolling, it was too much of a hassle for me to go out. I knew that I'd probably pass out. Better to do that on my couch than in some parking lot. It was a lot easi-er—and cheaper—to stay home and let the drugs, the booze, and the party come to me. Which it did, as the day wore on.

Once in a while I would hit a local bar. I remember one time, Larry and one of his buddies asked me to meet them for lunch. I arrived and had the bartender line 'em up: two double shots of Southern Comfort, double vodka and cran-berry juice, and a glass of water. No food. Larry's friend looked at my little assembly line of self-destruction and said to Larry in a stage whisper that I could hear: "Are you kid-ding me? This is his lunch?"

Whether I was working at some stupid, menial job or not, by the afternoon I had to get to work—my real work: Lying. Lying is a big part of the addict's life. Don't look disgusted. In this sense, we're in good company—lawyers, politicians, corporate spokespeople all lie, too. The fact that I spent hours a day lying is probably one of the few things I had in com-mon with your typical American corporate drone. Sometimes, of course, they have to lie for a good reason. An addict's lying involves trying to convince everybody that he doesn't have what they know he'd do anything to get: Drugs. This was the 1980s, and our big drug was coke.

Coke, of course, was incredibly expensive, which is one

reason that the cheaper smoked form called crack really caught on, with devastating effects, in poor neighborhoods. I smoked crack many times, but generally my preferred mode of getting coke into my body was through the nose. Indeed, I had progressed my way up the middle-class white man's coke hierarchy. I started by snorting a couple of lines in high school. Typical of an addict like me, I was soon buying what we called "sixteenths" (a sixteenth of an ounce), then "eight-balls"—an eighth of an ounce, or three grams, which in those days cost about two hundred and fifty bucks. By the time I moved into the apartment, at age twenty-one, my standard coke denomination was a quarter ounce. Anything less was like, *Why bother?* A quarter ounce of coke cost about seven hundred dollars and it would last me a weekend. Not exactly your most economical form of recreation.

Given my need and its costs, I wanted as much coke for myself as possible. So a large part of the lying was trying to convince my various girlfriends and other male and female druggie friends that I didn't have any. "Hey, man," I'd say when they'd call or show up. "I did it all last night." Then I'd reach into the back of my desk drawer, pull out the gram I had saved, roll out my special snorter, and give it a few toots.

Oh yes, I had all the accoutrements for successful coke use:

I used a gold razor blade to cut up the coke. In high school I'd used the barrel of a Bic pen to snort my lines. Now that I was a cool adult, I used more elaborate methods. For a while, I did the cliché of a rolled-up hundred dollar bill. Eventually I used a glass cocaine snorter, designed for the connoisseur addict like me. It had a U-shaped piece you could stick into each nostril and Hoover up every grain. The centerpiece of my little coke den was a sixteen by twenty inch glass-framed picture of Mötley Crüe. It had a flat surface—perfect for cutting up the coke—with a half-inch indentation separating the glass from the wooden frame, perfect for catching every stray, expensive flake.

I never used a mirror to cut it up. I didn't want to look at myself while I was snorting.

So I'd sit there by myself and crank up the stereo. When I was all excited and wired up, and maybe had a few friends around, it was hair metal all the way through the early evening: Crüe, AC/DC, Guns 'N Roses, Poison. Later, when the crowd left, it was moodier stuff: James Taylor, Lionel Ritchie, Cat Stevens, and my favorite melancholy ballad, "Angie" by the Stones. These were sad and lonely times. I liked being around people when I was stoned, but I didn't want to share any of the stuff I was getting stoned with. My lies about not having any coke kept people away (except for the women I needed as sexual partners). Such a dilemma for the poor addict.

The dishonesty was also a big part of my "second" job: small-time drug dealer. I got my drugs from three midlevel suppliers: Matt, a good friend of mine, Barry, a friend of the girl who used to cut my hair, and Ferd—my former hockey teammate, who had gone to become a real Ohio narco king. Ferd was probably moving close to a hundred pounds of pot and half a kilo of coke every week. They'd usually drop the stuff off with me, although occasionally I met Matt in the parking lot of a department store to get the coke, which made me nervous. I was always expecting it to go down like some movie or cop TV show, where the minute we exchange the drugs and money, you hear somebody yell, "Let's go!," feet clomping, and the next thing you know I'm spread-eagled up against my car. Fortunately, for me, that never happened.

I only bought eight-balls from these guys, but I was a regular customer—so regular that Barry the dealer wanted to cut me off. I was like, "What? Cut me off? This is your job, dude." He said, "I don't want to see you kill yourself." You know you're in bad shape when your drug dealer is concerned about how much you're using.

So I'd buy an eight-ball from one of my dealers; then I'd take three quarters of it for myself and sell the rest as a full eight-ball. Buying drugs isn't like buying a new car; there aren't government or industry standards that have to be adhered to. I say it's an eight-ball, you don't think so, fine . . . don't buy it. Lots of other people around here will. This is the middle of Ohio, not uptown Manhattan, pal. Your choices are limited. (This was not actually true. You could drive fifteen minutes to Toledo and score all you wanted, but that was a black neighborhood, and a lot of these middle-American kids were too scared to do that. Not too scared to do drugs, however.)

The fun part of dealing, besides the fact that I had all this coke for my head, was that I could play Scarface and sit around with a load of coke piled up on my living room table. I'd build it up like a little snow mountain, and watch some of my so-called friends watch me as I took big, deep snorts. They'd be licking their lips and I'd say, "Hey, you want some, you gotta buy some." One time, I told a group of deadbeats who had come by to score, that I had to take a leak. I got up and left my white mountain on the table. It was a ruse. I peeked back around the corner of my living room, and saw one of them pick up my rolled up bill and try to take a quick snort. I rushed back in the room, ripped the bill out of his hand, and punched him in the mouth (I never hesitated with that stuff—between hockey and addiction, I was probably in more fights than some professional boxers). Then I threw his ass out on the street. This sent a good message: Don't fuck with the coke dealer.

I was pretty good at getting what I wanted: I once convinced some local dirtbag to rob the house of a guy I grew up with, in order to get drug money. He broke in, stole a video cassette recorder, came back to me lugging the thing. The plan was to hock it—a VCR, for Chrissakes; how much did we really think we were going to get for it?—and then spend the money on drugs. I stuck it in my old hockey bag and gave it a girl I knew for safekeeping. She called the cops. They came to my parents' house—I was there at the time—arrested me on the spot, and dragged me out in handcuffs. At the station, I was told that I was looking at eight years for receiving stolen property. They offered me a deal. If I could give them "information" on the local drug scene, maybe they could reduce the sentence. What they were interested in, they said, was the purity of the cocaine circulating in the Toledo area. They wanted me to make a coke buy—something, they seemed to realize, I was very experienced at—and then bring them a sample. Now, this was my idea of law and order! "Sure," I said, "I'm happy to do my duty as a citizen." So they give me two hundred dollars and off I went to Point Place, a part of Toledo where you could buy any kind of drug you wanted. I bought a couple of grams from a street-corner dealer and immediately had to test it myself. I did one line— and couldn't stop. Within a few minutes, almost all the coke I had purchased (with the cops' money) was gone. I drove back to Sylvania and walked into the police station high as a kite. I sat there as the detectives examined the remaining and rather minuscule sample I had brought them. I tried to look serious, but inside I was grinning like the Cheshire Cat. Did the cops know I'd basically ripped them off . . . that I'd used their money to score and get high? Did they care? I'm not sure—but it sure was fun to think that I'd pulled one over on them. Not to mention the fact that the charges against me for receiving stolen property were dropped.

By that point, I had moved to Granny's. Dad had finally had enough of what was going on at his apartment. I thought I had fooled him, but I hadn't. He just came up to the apartment and looked around. He'd check the dumpster out back and see that it was full of liquor bottles, cans, and little clear plastic bags. He'd see me, and know I was coked—because the pupils of my eyes would be black and dilated.

My little addict's nest came undone on March 6, 1991. He came up to the apartment and said, "You have two options. Either you're out on the street or in rehab. Either way, it's over here. I'm not going to watch you kill yourself in my apartment."

I said, "I'll take rehab . . . but only after I finish this cocaine." I wanted the bad stuff to stop at this point, I really did, but I wasn't quite ready to give it up. So my dad sat there for eight hours, while I finished off an entire quarter ounce of coke. It was bizarre. There were moments when he'd cry; then he'd matter-of-factly discuss what they would do with the insurance money he'd collect when I finally overdosed and died (he said they'd probably donate it to a charity that fights substance abuse).

After eight hours he took me to the local Sylvania medical center, Flower Hospital, which had a rehab unit. I spent two weeks there. It amounted to a two-week break when I could eat well, sleep undisturbed, avoid people I owed money to, and listen to some interesting lectures. The minute I got out, however, it was back to business. Within three days of leaving rehab I started drinking again. That night I got a bunch of tranquilizers, took them at my friend's house, and ended up passing out in his living room with his parents sitting there. Next morning, I woke up on their floor, in my underwear. Something wasn't right, and I realized that I had soiled myself. I took off my underwear, threw it in their backyard, put my pants back on, and started drinking again.

When you pass out in someone's house nearly naked and defecate on yourself, you've just about hit bottom, in my opinion. But I wasn't done yet.

First, I needed a new place to stay. Whenever I was really scared, really in trouble, or really desperate for money or sympathy, I went down the road to Grandma's. Lillian Ward was and is a strong person, an absolutely critical person in my life. She knew the score about me—and wasn't denying the fact that I was an addict, something that others, including my parents, were.

I moved in there in early April 1991, and the debauchery continued. Many nights I remember puking in her toilet; she'd come in, stand behind me, and pat me on the back, saying "I know you are going to beat this someday." And I was lying there on her bathroom floor, my arms wrapped around the toilet seat, saying, "I'm dying, Grandma. I'm not going to beat it . . . it's killing me." And she would insist that yes, I would beat it. Eventually, Granny would be instrumental in my recovery. But before then, even her reassuring words couldn't bring me out of the dark spiral that my life was becoming. No doubt at this point my entire life was "a bad day," but some were worse than others. One of the very worst was Thanksgiving Day 1991, when I strung together three of the most strung-out days of my life.

The day before Thanksgiving is a big drinking night for a lot of people—especially drunks like me. But this year, I had something really special in the works. You see, this weekend my grandma was out of town; I was going to mind the house while she was away, and I had a nice little Thanksgiving surprise all planned out. I was going to get really wasted, throw the mother of all parties, then go into her garage, close the door, get in the car, turn on the ignition, and kill myself. I remember going around town that morning—I even went to the gym; guess I wanted to look buff for the coroner—seeing a lot of familiar faces, and thinking, *This is the last time you're going to see these people.* After my workout, it was straight to the liquor store, which opened at 10 A.M. that day; I bought two half gallons of vodka and was hammered by 11. As usual, Larry—a good guy, whose friendship I totally abused for my own selfish, addicted purposes—came by, but because this was my grandma's house and not my apartment, he stopped to take in the view: Her backyard faces Ten Mile Creek. The view from Grandma's back porch is almost idyllic: a lazy river, surrounded by walnut, maple, and buckeye trees, and a dazzling array of flowers. "Nice view," Larry said.

"Screw that," I remember telling him. I was planning to check out that day, and no bullshit view was going to distract me.

I was waiting for my drugs to arrive—I had about three hundred dollars in cash set out for a quarter ounce of coke. I'm still not sure what happened, and neither is Larry, but a group of our friends arrived, we were drinking, more people came and went—this was the middle of the afternoon—and at some point, I realized my money was gone. No coke. In retrospect, that might have saved my life, because if I'd stayed awake, all coked up, instead of passing out, I probably would have gone through with the plan. Some of what happened is a blur, but I do know that by evening, having continued to drink, I was talking about burning my grandma's house down with all of us in it. I was obviously so drunk, I'd forgotten about the original suicide plan.

For dinner that night, I made a cocktail in the blender that my grandma used to serve all the time: pineapples, strawberries, yogurt, and a banana, all blended up together—what today you'd call a "smoothie." Except the addict added a special ingredient, the one Grandma left out of her recipes: A half a quart of vodka. By 9 P.M. (so Larry later told me) I was passed out. I woke up the next morning, still drunk. I was naked in my bed, with one girl fully clothed lying next to me, and another—looking none too happy—standing there staring at us. The two girls started to fight. I reached out and tried to pull both of 'em on top of me for a little three way sex, but I was too hammered and they were too angry. They stormed out of the room, and as I began to think about it, I realized that I had gotten too fucked up the night before to kill myself. Imagine that. I couldn't even pull that off, I was so wasted. What a loser. *Well,* I thought, *today's Thanksgiving. If I do it today, everybody in this town will be thanking me.*

The girls were gone, my three hundred dollars was gone, and I was still here. I was not happy. One answer for that: I called Clips, the liquor store, to see if they were open. When they answered, I was jumping up and down, so excited was I that they were open on Thanksgiving Day (in retrospect, I think they might have opened up just for me). I got ever-faithful Larry to drive me to Clips; we picked up more booze, stopping first at Sears, where I used my grandma's credit card to get a cash advance. By noon that day I was out of my mind again and alone—but still without any cocaine. The normal people had all gone home for Thanksgiving. My parents were having Thanksgiving dinner at their house just a couple of miles away, but I wanted no part of it. So I just sat in my grandma's living room, mixing drink after drink. By four o'clock that afternoon, I decided it was time to kill myself. I remember getting up to get into my grandma's car. But I must have chickened out at the last minute. The next thing I knew, I was waking up in my girlfriends' bed at her parents' house (some boyfriend I was: I had attempted to sleep with at least two other girls in the preceding twenty-four hours). Evidently, I had driven the car out of my grandma's garage and over to Jenny's house, where I drove it up on the front lawn. I got out, left the car running, walked in the house in the middle of their dinner, and before saying a word passed out on their floor. They all sat there over their Thanksgiving dinner, forks poised in midair, mouths agape. So I am told.

Here I was now, waking up for my third straight day of debauchery—and one more chance for a successful suicide. After tearfully dishonest apologies to my girlfriend and her mother for ruining their Thanksgiving dinner, it was back to my grandma's house. I arrived to find the front and garage doors wide open and music blaring. Another buddy, also named Todd, was sitting there. He told me he'd found the house like this late the night before, and decided he'd better stay and keep an eye on it. He told me that when he arrived, the Doors' song "The End" was playing over and over on the CD. That was by design, I recalled as he told me the story. It was going to be the soundtrack of my suicide. But again, I'd fucked that up, just like everything else. Here I was. Still alive.

Oh well, let's party.

Which we did. Finally, at about 3 P.M., with me drunk out of my skull, my buddy Matt the dealer showed up with the quarter ounce of coke I'd been coveting since Wednesday. For the rest of the weekend, I did lines, puked, got laid a couple of times—once with Larry watching (but not with my girlfriend; she wanted no part of me for a while). At one point in the evening, I punched a girl: Kim was her name, and we had known each other awhile. I was sitting on the couch with Kim's buddy Kris, and I started fondling her. I did it right in front of Kim, and she didn't take kindly to my provocation. She picked a beer bottle and threw at me, hitting me square in the face. I got up and clocked her right in the face. She had a black eye for months—something I am definitely not proud of.

At another point, a couple of hockey players showed up.

They were both in college by then, a little younger than me, but they'd gone to Sylvania High School when I was the man: the goalie no one scored on. They remembered me as Todd, the best high school goalie in the state and the guy with pro potential. Now I was Todd, the worst drunk and drug addict in town, and the guy with no future.

I remember looking up from Grandma's table as I did yet another line and catching one of them staring at me, with a horrified expression on his face. Even in my haze and rage, I felt ashamed.

By Sunday afternoon of that Thanksgiving weekend, I had consumed, over five days, about three gallons of vodka, a case of beer, the better part of an ounce of pot, and a full quarter ounce of coke. About 6 P.M., I realized I had to pick up Granny at the airport. I sprang up on wobbly legs, shooed all the drunks out, and started assessing the damage. There were empty bottles, booze stains, and grains of coke scattered on the rug (those I sucked up immediately). There was also a porno video stuck in the VCR, a former girlfriend's sex toy was missing—left somewhere in her house; not in her bedroom, I hoped—and, inexplicably, a missing toothbrush. In a coke-fueled frenzy, I cleaned up the house, got in the car, and pulled up to the terminal as Granny was getting off the plane.

I can only imagine how I looked: bloodshot eyes, trembling hands, reeking of booze; plus I had a fat lip from being smacked by the beer bottle by the girl. Grandma hugged me, looked at me, and said, "What happened?"

For once, I told the truth—or at least most of it. I tearfully begged Grandma to forgive me. Then I called Jenny and asked her to do the same—the second time in three days. That was a bravura performance. And of course, it was a lie. I had no intention of quitting and every intention of attempting suicide again. A few days off and I was back to my normal routine. It would go on and on, day after day, for another year.

In my 20s, losing myself in the lifestyle of drugs and alcohol.

Not my finest hour: one of my several arrests.

5

Guns and Roses

During my last year of addiction my grandmother knew what was going on, all right (after the Thanksgiving Day orgy, how could she not?), but she also remained steadfast in her belief that I was going to survive.

I wasn't so sure.

One evening I was at the apartment of a guy named Nick, a friend I had met during my brief time as a student at the University of Toledo. He brought along a girl named Kathy. As was often the case when I was involved, things deteriorated as I drank and drank. Part of this was told to me later by Nick and Kathy, but apparently at one point, while they were out of the room, I went rooting around and found the nine-millimeter handgun Nick kept in his home for protection. The pistol was loaded—and so was I.

He and Kathy returned to find me sitting on the couch with the barrel of the gun in my mouth, my finger on the trigger. I took it out, smiled at them, and put it back in. At that point, Nick grabbed the gun out of my hand. When Kathy told me the story later, she said it was one of scariest and saddest moments of her life. Scary, because she realized that had Nick not taken action, I very well might have splattered my brains all over his apartment. Sad, because she began to glimpse the depths of depression and pain I must have felt to reach such a point.

I had guns on my mind for a while after that. At one point I contacted a guy I knew who could get me a gun cheap. I told him I needed it for self-defense. He came by Granny's one night when I was wasted, and I told him something about how this would be great to use to blow my head off. But I couldn't come through with the scratch. No money, no mind-blowing gun. Being broke that night might have saved my life.

Would I have pulled the trigger if I had been able to buy that gun . . . or if Nick hadn't pulled it out of my hands at his apartment? To this day, I'm not sure. I had reached the nadir of my addiction and self-loathing. On the other hand, it is precisely at these times—when things seem as if they can get no worse—that addicts begin to turn the corner. Maybe it's because we can feel ourselves touching bottom and recognize that either we must now rise or die. Maybe it's a self-defense mechanism, whereby the last vestige of rational thought in the brain summons up its strength for one final cry: *Stop!*

Or maybe it's just weariness.

Whatever the reasons, at just about the point where I felt I could get no more depraved, no more depressed, things began to turn around.

It was April 12, 1993—early spring in the Midwest. I was working for a construction contractor at the time. I had spent the day at work in a hot, cramped garage, tearing up a cement floor with a jackhammer. That afternoon, when I got home from work, I started drinking, as usual. To celebrate my dad's birthday (although hardly in the manner that he would have approved of), I hit the bottle extra hard. The next morning, I remember groggily looking outside, seeing the sun rising over Ten Mile Creek behind Granny's house. It was going to be a beautiful day. Too nice for me to work, I decided.

Instead, I decided to devote my full attention to inebriation. I kept drinking right though the day and into the evening, when some of friends of mine and I had tickets to see Guns 'N Roses in Detroit. We drank, we snorted blow, and for good measure, I took some pills on the way to the arena that night. At some point between Axl Rose's first shimmy and scream and Slash's final power chord of the night, I blacked out. My friends found me after the show, passed out outside of the arena with no shirt on, my pants unbuttoned, leaning up against a pole with a girl next to me.

I awoke the next morning, got in my car and drove to a local bar. From ten thirty to noon, I downed one shot after another. Then I got into my car and started driving aimlessly around Sylvania. Suddenly I felt my car lurch. Craning my neck out the window, I could see I had a flat tire. I pulled over at a local Jiffy Lube, asked to use the phone, and called my buddy Larry to have him come pick me up. While doing so, I pulled my pants down and urinated all over the manager's desk.

You never saw people move so fast . . . even in a Jiffy Lube. Customers scattered, mechanics ran over from the service area to see what was happening, and the manager called the cops. I blew a .284 blood alcohol level—well over the legal limit—and they promptly arrested me. The cops also know that I was doing more than drinking. "Where are the drugs, Todd?" one officer asked me.

"I took 'em all," I replied.

The cops slapped me with a DUI, impounded my car, and put me in a holding cell. Larry, who had showed up in time to witness the fracas at the Jiffy Lube, followed us down to the police station and eventually was able to bail me out. As I left, I groused to the cops for not letting me take the six-pack of Moosehead Beer that had been in my car. Larry took me back to Granny's, where I got back on the phone to ask another friend to pick up some booze and come over. This guy showed up a little later with a fifth of vodka, beer, and— oh boy—crack.

It was during that night that I had, finally, that moment of self-discovery that I had been waiting for since I slugged down that first sip of beer and the following scotch—poison for someone with my risk factors—back in the eight grade. Why did it happen then? No one knows. Why did it not happen earlier in my life as an addict, or later? No one knows that either. But it did happen then, thank goodness. Sadly, not all addicts are so fortunate. With it happening, suddenly I was on the road to recovery, even though I only barely realized it at the time. I was surely lucky that I did realize it.

Addicts who are going to recover do have to, as some level, be ready for the realization that they really want to stop, must stop, if and when it does come.

I drank and smoked most of it on and off through the rest of that night. As the night went on, my disgust over what had transpired the previous two days grew and grew. However, instead of sentencing myself to slow death by poison—my usual, self-loathing response—this time I slowly began to turn the anger toward the poison itself, toward the alcohol and drugs, and my inability to deal with them. That was the real problem, I began to see. If I could control that, I could control my life. And I wanted life, I realized, not death. Despite all my dramatic gunplay, despite the drunken, over-wrought speeches about how I wished my mother had taken me with her, what I really wanted was to go on living. I want-ed to feel good, have a sense of purpose, start a healthy rela-tionship, build a career. I was tired of being perceived (by myself, as well as others) as a loser, a drunk, a troublemaker. Understand, of course, that this realization came fitfully, over five or six hours. I cursed the booze as I was sipping it. Still, the sips got farther and fewer as the night wore on, like an engine of self-destruction slowly running out of steam.

The next morning a strange but soothing feeling came over

me, different from the bitter, melancholy state I usually found myself in near the end of a long binge. At around that time, my grandmother came down and sat down quietly next to me. It was almost as if she knew instinctively that something important was going to happen . . . something besides me puking or passing out . . . and wanted to be there to support me. At about noon on April 15, 1993, I drained my glass of beer and declared, "I don't want this anymore. I am done."

I knew at that moment I had taken my last drink; knew it with the same savage conviction that had kept me drinking and taking drugs relentlessly for the previous thirteen years. The addictive energy had been rerouted, almost as if a circuit switch had been flipped in my brain. Now I was suddenly passionate and determined to get sober, and stay that way. The fog of about twelve hours—or was it all thirteen years?—of drinking began to dissipate. I was rational, I was clear. I had just taken my first tentative step on the road to recovery.

Some might say it was high time, pardon the pun: I had nothing at this point. No money, no family except Granny, and only a few real friends. My credit was ruined, I was in poor health, I had no job, no future at all. What I did have was a full heart. This is what you must have to achieve sobriety: the desire to do what you must in order to get and remain sober. I wasn't quite sure what that would entail yet, but already I was confident that I could achieve it.

I was not alone in this: In 2005 the National Institute on Alcohol Abuse and Alcoholism reported on a study that found more than one-third—35 percent—of U.S. adults with alcoholism are in recovery. I don't know how many of them made the decision in quite the same circumstances I did—after a three-day binge that included a stint in jail, not to mention a heavy-metal concert—but that doesn't matter. It's a point often overlooked by our society that many, many alcoholics and drug abusers can and do recover, and go on to lead successful lives.

A lot of them have been helped by 12-step programs, such as Alcoholics Anonymous, although—as I would discover later—there are other recovery tools, techniques and approaches that can be successfully used as well. My first stop after I had decided to stop was the local AA chapter. I didn't need to look it up in the phone book. I had been there before. Like many addicts, I had been ordered to AA meetings to avoid further jail time during some of my earlier scrapes with the law. Some respond well to being force-fed into the program. I didn't. I remember sitting in the meetings and thinking what a drag it was, how boring: who cared what these old, dried-up drunks had to say. Also, it bothered me how many of them were puffing on cigarettes, and how choked with smoke the room was. "I don't need to get lung cancer to quit drinking," I groused to a friend at the time.

In sum, I felt uncomfortable at AA the couple of times I had been compelled to go. Then again I had felt uncomfortable almost everyplace in my life up to that point, save maybe a bar stool or in front of some lines of coke.

This time was different. I couldn't wait to get back to AA, smoke or no. This time I was eager to learn everything I could from this, the original 12-step program. For once, I shut my mouth, watched and listened to what these people had to say, and how they had managed to achieve sobriety in their lives. I had heard some of the AA canon before—about admitting your powerlessness over alcohol, about believing in something greater than yourself—but now it was making sense. I wanted what these people had—sobriety, a new life—and so I hung on every word.

In a 12-step meeting, lots of people talk and share their experiences. Although I tried to learn something from everyone there, I wasn't quite as interested in the casual user or the yuppie whose drinking got a little out of hand. In AA—and soon in the related 12-step meetings for cocaine users that I began attending—I was interested in the real hard-core addicts; in people like me. So that I could say, *Okay, he was a mess like I am now, but he recovered . . . and so can I.*

Such a guy was Carl, whom I met in a Cocaine Anonymous meeting. Carl was an older blue-collar guy, not some three-piece-suit businessman who had developed a fondness for the blow and had to attend these meetings to save his six-figure job or because a judge had ordered him to. In the past Carl had screwed up as badly as I had, and for as long as I had. When Carl spoke, there was no b.s., no sob stories, and no excuses. But there *was* hope. Carl talked about a newfound confidence in himself, about a lengthy sobriety, about a life that had improved, about new friends (or at least non-using friends), about a life in which drugs did not play a part. I was drawn to this. I remember sitting there one night listening to him, and it almost seemed as if he was sketching out a road map for me. "Life doesn't have to be this way," he said. "You can beat the addiction. I did it, you can, too."

I began to realize that he was right. But to do that, I also had to understand it. As the days went on, a few things became clearer to me. I could see that in many ways, the ongoing dissolution was—in addition to whatever genetic traits I possessed—due in large part to my desire to throw myself my own little "pity party." I was feeling sorry for myself; angry about my mother and my family situation, and later angry and ashamed at being kicked off the team and out of school. And the party just kept going on and feeding itself. I was getting drunk and high out of self-pity and embarrassment over things I had done while I was getting drunk and high. A stupid, as well as vicious, cycle. I began to see this pattern, and I recognized that having a drink or snorting some blow was not going to make anything better, just worse.

In AA I also learned that it was okay to admit powerlessness. A lot of addicts are full of bravado. I certainly was. The more poison I could put into my body, the better, I always thought. I could handle it. I was in control of it. Of course, I was not. My life was desperately out of control. That's what had led me to these meetings. I faced the fact that the alcohol and the drugs had won. I remember in one meeting, someone had said, "How many times do you have to get your butt kicked by Mike Tyson to realize you're not going to beat him?" As an ex-athlete, that made a lot of sense to me. It was a fine line between determination and futility; between trying my best to defend the net against Wayne Gretzky and admitting that he was just too fast for me to stop.

Alcohol had KO'ed me, shut me down, sent me to the

showers, embarrassed me the way Gretzky would have on the ice or Tyson would have in the ring. That was a hard thing for me to accept, but doing so was a big step toward recovery.

Gradually, over the course of that spring and summer, things began to come together for me. I was beginning to learn the truth of what I tell addicts today: Recovery is like building a house—you don't start with the roof, you start with a solid foundation. That solid foundation is getting sober.

As with everything else in my life, I jumped into sobriety with both feet. In addition to the meetings, I had the support of good friends, such as Robin. Robin had been there; she was a recovering addict and very active in local support groups. I knew her and I trusted her. Robin became my own support group. She'd come over to my grandmother's house—a much quieter and healthier place since I had put down that last beer—and we'd talk for hours about life without drugs and alcohol and how to attain it. I also read a lot about recovery and the various theories of how and why people become addicts. This was fascinating to me; as if I were reading an owner's manual for my own head.

Of course, even those of us trying to build a new life still have to deal with the ramifications of the old one. That summer I went to court for my third DUI charge, the "Jiffy

Lube incident" that had helped spark my recovery. The judge listened as my attorney explained that I had been attending AA meetings, and that I was serious about sobriety. Then again, he'd probably heard the same things from lots of other addicts who were then back in his court in a few months, this time having robbed or killed someone. He sentenced me to three days in jail, thirty-three days of work release—which meant that I did some menial job during the day, and then slept in jail at night—a one-year suspension of my driver's license, plus a year's probation.

The last part of the sentence I didn't mind. They could have made the probation twenty years for all I cared; I knew in my heart I was done with my old way of living. But jail sucked. For my three-day incarceration I was sent to the Corrections Center of Northwest Ohio in Stryker, a town in the western part of the state near the Indiana border. My first night there, I was going through the food line for dinner. As I was getting my mashed potatoes slopped down on my plate, the guy behind the counter said "Hey Todd, how you doing?" I looked up and saw that this fellow inmate was an old drug buddy of mine. *Man,* I thought, *it's a bad situation when people in jail start recognizing you.*

While I had confidence that I was now on the road to

beating my addiction, others were skeptical. As I was leaving Stryker, my three-day sentence served, one of the guards called out to me, "Hey Todd, we'll see you again soon."

I stiffened up when I heard that, turned around, and said to him coolly and very slowly, in my best *read my lips* voice: "You will never see me here again."

And they haven't.

The second phase of my incarceration was thirty-three days at the Lucas County Work Release Program in Toledo. During the day I spent my time pushing a broom in a warehouse alone and bored out of my mind. At night I was back in jail, listening to the snoring and mutterings of fifty other miscreants. I'd wake up there in the morning, eat breakfast there, shower there. It was degrading and humiliating to go back to this situation every night. I kept sane for that month by telling myself that I wouldn't have to do this stuff forever, I was paying for my mistakes.

It was particularly hard when my dad came to visit. He and I had plenty of problems in our relationship, between my mother's suicide and her "role" in my addiction, not to mention the problems I had caused him and his second wife. It would take years to sort things out with both Terry Crandell and my stepmother. Like any parent-child relationship, there's guilt, anger, baggage. Given what happened with my mother, and everything I later put my father and step-mother through, you can just imagine the size of the Crandell family's baggage train.

Not long after I was released from the work program, I decided I wanted to return to school. I went back to the judge and asked for driving privileges so that I could attend classes at the University of Toledo. He looked at my attendance record at the AA and Cocaine Anonymous meetings, read the glowing reports from my probation officer, and, I think, saw that I was serious about sobriety. He agreed to my request, and I was able to drive to classes. Because I was so wedded to a program of self-improvement in every aspect of my life, college was a godsend; a key part in my striving to become a "normal" person. *This is what sober people do, this is what people who don't have a thirteen-year history of addiction do,* I thought. *They go to school, they work, they get a job.*

Classes were fun and challenging—a far cry from pushing a broom. Also, for the first time, I was hearing things, at school and in the meetings, with a clear head. This is something people who are not continually drunk or stoned may not appreciate. Think about how you might feel when you have the flu or have just came out of anesthesia. This is more or the less the state I had walked around in for thirteen years.

Now the fog was lifted. I was hearing, seeing, and understanding things with a new perceptiveness. In addition to learning about marketing channels and sales management, I learned how to use a computer, I learned how to type: basic life skills for what was basically a new life. In the spring of 1994 I completed that associate degree in sales and marketing. I was really proud, and was ready to take the next step in my recovery.

The judge knew about my sincere efforts to straighten out, but a lot of others didn't. That was deliberate. I did not tell everybody that I had stopped drinking, as I had a couple of times in the past, when my sobriety lasted about seventy-two hours. This time, I decided I would let my actions speak for me. Believe me, my actions needed a good spokesperson. I'd angered and hurt a lot of people, damaged a lot of relationships over the years. On April 15, 1994—one year to the day after I put down that last beer—I called my friend Kevin, who grew up in Sylvania and had known me through the years. I said, "Hey, I'm a year sober today." He said, "Big deal. Let me know you have five." It was a necessary slap in the face. He wasn't trying to dismiss my efforts at staying sober. What he was saying was: *You're sober for a year; you were a raging, drunk, out-of-control lunatic for thirteen years. So you've still got a long way to go to earn our trust back.* The comment stung at first. But he was right. I still had a lot to prove, a lot to learn.

One of the key lessons was the importance of help. They tell you that right away in AA meetings. You need support, you need help. This went against the cocky Crandell grain. Help? Goalies didn't need help. They did it on their own, man-against-man on the ice. But over the course of my first year of sobriety, I realized that I did need help, beyond even what my friends and support group members could provide.

Help arrived in the form of a beautiful blonde wearing a white T-shirt with a yellow sunflower on it.

She was sitting on the sofa in the apartment of a girl I happened to be dating. The girl introduced me to Melissa, and I knew in an instant I was in love. Melissa was from Huntsville, Ohio, and had come to Toledo to attend the university. When I met her, she was contemplating moving back to Huntsville because her lease was almost up. She liked hockey, she was a good listener, and, although a bit shy, she was rock-solid in her support of me and what I was doing. It took awhile—we were both dating other people at the time we met—but eventually I got the nerve to ask her out. Our dates were pretty tame. I remember we'd watch a lot of TV together; *Melrose Place* was our favorite. While I was powerfully attracted to her, my goal wasn't to get her into bed at the first possible moment, which had been the case with most of the other women I'd dated. I just liked her company. She heard my life story, listened to my confessions about my anguish, about my mother, about how I'd basically tried to kill myself for thirteen years, and she didn't flinch. Unlike a lot of other people, Melissa wasn't hung up on what I'd done in my past but rather, what I was going to do in my future.

I knew that future had to include her. As we dated, I began to behave like the gentleman I never had been in previous relationships. I even brought her roses from time to time. On December 23, 1995, a year and a half after my last drink, I proposed to her in the front seat of my Honda Civic. She said yes, and it was the closest feeling I'd had to a buzz since my final bender.

6

Back on the Ice

I can see him as the play begins to develop on the other end of the ice. It's . . . Sergei Fedorov? Mike Bossy? No, wait . . . it's Gretzky! He's got the puck and he's sweeping past our defensemen, skating in and out with that unbelievable grace, the smoothness that gave him his sobriquet, the Great One. He's across the blue line now, gaining speed and getting ready to take the shot. With less than a minute left and his team down by one goal, he's thinking *score*. The crowd knows it and begins to roar. I can sense them standing up in the seats behind where I am, defending this lonely little outpost that's now about to become the center of attention for twenty thousand fans packed into the arena. Nothing can stop

Gretzky now, but me. I see his cold blue eyes—he may be a nice guy off the ice, but not here—and those eyes are staring right at me. In a nanosecond he's sizing me up, wondering exactly which angle to take. He feints right, and then his stick is a blur, then—bam!—the puck comes flying toward the left side of the net. Like in a movie, I see it happening in slow motion. He fooled me, that bastard. I went for the fake. Sending out an all points bulletin to every neural pathway in my body, recruiting every muscle fiber I have, I stop and lurch my body back in the other direction, extending my arm as far as I can—and *thump,* I feel the puck, caught right in the center of my glove.

Shot blocked! Gretzky denied! Crandell saves it! The Great One bangs his stick on the ice in anger as he skates past me. My teammates are going crazy—and there's the buzzer. It's over. We win!

About that time is when I usually wake up from the dream. For years, even during my addiction, I had this dream, or one like it. Me back in goal, making the great moves, making the athletic saves, saving my team's ass . . . again! During the drunk years, it just took the old morning puke to remind me that it was all a dream, and that I was as far away from being ready to go back to hockey as a guy in the tropics is from making a snowman. But now, in 1994, the situation was different than it had been five or ten years earlier. After thirteen years of addiction, I had been sober for almost a year. I'd attended my meetings, and I had kept it together. I was twenty-eight, so the idea of playing in the NHL—a real possibility when I was a teenager back in Juniors, before I fucked everything up—was long gone. Still, I had the dream, and I knew somehow that despite skills and instincts that had been dulled by a decade of drugs and booze, I could still play.

Maybe Larry read my mind that December day when we were sitting around his apartment, trying to fill time the way I did in the first few months after my sobriety. "D'ya ever think about playing goal again, Todd?" he asked, out of the blue. "Hell, yes," I admitted. "But I don't have any equipment." I didn't mention the fact that I was also lacking in conditioning, flexibility, skating ability, and reaction time— which means I was lacking, period. Larry, God bless him, must have known this was eating inside me. "C'mon," he said. "Let's go to Perani's." Perani's! It had been a long time since I'd even contemplated a trip there. Located in downtown Detroit, home of the Red Wings (then an also-ran, now Stanley Cup champs), Perani's was hockey heaven—where players from all over the upper Midwest went to get their stuff. They had every kind of goalie equipment known to man, and any man who plays goalie needs equipment. By the time I was done—a pair of flat-bladed goalie skates, thirty-one-inch-high knee pads, chest protector and arm pads, a blocker and catching mit, Sherwood stick, goalie mask—I had spent two thousand dollars of Larry's money.

I needed every bit of it. Goaltender is a tough position; one of the toughest in any sport. The goalie is immobile, vulnerable, and yet essential. He can't help his team win by scoring, but if he doesn't do his job, they lose the game. "An utterly thankless position," wrote George Plimpton when he spent a season as a goalie for the Boston Bruins, an experience he wrote about in his book, *Open Net*. He described it in his inimitable, Plimptonesque fashion: "Surely, [goaltender] is the most unglamorous position in sport. In appearance the goaltender resembles a bottle-shaped structure, stuffed as a strawman, and about as graceful. And of course, there was the danger—the thought of trying to handle an object, as solid as a bullet head, and coming in on one at speeds of up to 130 miles per hour. And then there was the indignity of being scored upon. There was perhaps nothing comparable in sports that showed off one's disgrace as much as a hockey puck lying spent in the nets behind the goaltender."

"Goalies have a very high-pressure job," says my friend Bruce MacDonald, who played with the Philadelphia Flyers. "A forward messes up, people don't really notice. A goalie makes a mistake and the puck's in the net." For that reason, Bruce says, "Goalies have always been known to be the nuts of the sport. They are usually a little more eccentric, free spirited."

That's me. I like the pressure; I like being at the center of attention. I like the game being on my shoulders. I don't necessarily like the fact that when I'm in goal, I'm restricted to the "crease"—the six-foot-long semicircle in front of the net. But I make up for it with my tattoos, my cool painted mask, and my *come on, let's see what you got* attitude. Besides, I can move pretty well back there.

Or at least I could when I was fourteen. Still, I'd had plenty of great moments on the ice as a teenager; I'd made some pretty nifty saves, and I'd sealed victories for my team. But that was all years ago; before the drugs and drinks took over my life.

Now, as I pulled on the gear at Perani's, I was wondering if I could still do it. Would I embarrass myself, fall on my ass on the ice, end up disgraced?

To find out, I went with Larry to the Sunday "old men's" hockey game at the local Sylvania rink. This was a purely recreational league, but a lot of former high school players participated. When I came in that night and the guys saw me putting on my goalie gear, there was a little buzz in the air. "Holy shit!" I heard somebody say. "TC is back in the net." This was the second of two games being played at the rink that night, and I noticed that some of the guys from the earlier game—many of whom I recognized—had decided to stick around to see if I could still play. Maybe some of them thought I was still a drunk, and would fall over comically on the ice.

I didn't say anything. I was nervous, but excited. It was the first time I'd been on the ice, standing in front of a net, in a decade.

I could feel my rustiness in the warm-ups, and in the first couple of shots taken at me. Fortunately, they were not close-range. As I scooped up the puck after one of them, I remember thinking that I was lucky, so far. Then . . . *smack!* A shot taken by my old friend Todd Weaver, from just outside the red circle to my right, came flying at me. It was a clear hard shot to the left side of the net; I just missed it. Goal. *Okay,* I thought. *I looked like shit on that one, but it won't happen again.*

It didn't.

As the minutes wore on that night, I could feel the old goalie within coming alive again. I began to be able to decipher the puck, determining what angle the shot was coming at, and could command my body to react in just the right place at just the right time. By the end of the night the puck looked like a giant beach ball coming at me in slow motion. Afterward, a lot of the local guys came around and thumped me on the shoulders. "You're back, TC," said one of them.

In a sense, I was: I was sober, straight, and back in front of the net.

Still, I had no illusions about my performance. I had been playing against local amateurs, guys around thirty years old. Inside me, the nagging question, the one that had lingered after every one of my hockey dreams, remained: Could I have made it in the NHL? Had I hooked on with the Juniors team in Detroit, could I—like others on that team—have eventually made it into the NHL?

Obviously, I'll never be able to answer the *What if?* part. But now that I was sober and back on the ice, I could at least rephrase the question:

Did I have the talent to play professionally?

Professional hockey exists in this country outside the

NHL. There's also the American Hockey League and the East Coast Hockey League, which, despite its name, is composed of thirty-one teams from Beaumont, Texas, to Bakersfield, California—and one near me, Toledo. The teams play a seventy-two-game schedule from October through April. While it is essentially the minor leagues of the sport, it's still "real" hockey; they play for pay. In fact, many NHL players have used the ECHL as a proving ground. I knew that at twenty-nine it was way too late for me to aspire to the NHL—but I could still take a shot at the ECHL.

First, I needed to get in shape. I started hitting the local gym, lifting weights. I began to go out and run: two or three miles a couple of times a week. I joined a summer hockey league, this one a notch or two higher than the "old-men's" group. There I ran into Glen Mears, who had played at Bowling Green University. He and Bruce MacDonald started working out with me. I think they were impressed by the fact that I was trying to make a comeback from addiction. Little did they know that I still was addicted—this time, to hockey. Soon the game had become my whole life again. Every spare moment I had was devoted to working out, watching games, or practicing my goalie skills. My feeling was that this had been the great love of my life as a kid; it had been taken away from me—largely because of my own misdeeds, partially because of my dad's opposition—and now I had it back. I knew it wouldn't be for long; I had no illusions about supporting the family that my fiancée, Melissa, and I planned to start on a semipro hockey player's game stipends. So I really felt a sense of urgency. This was my last opportunity to fashion my own little miracle on ice.

Bruce was able to get me invited to an exclusive, pro conditioning camp in Montreal. Most of the sixty guys invited to attend this five-day camp were already pros, many in the NHL. This was the real deal: Montreal, the "capital" of hockey and the home of the greatest team ever, the Canadiens; guys talking French in the locker room; players telling stories about going up against the big names in the sport. And there I was—a former crackhead. What was I doing here? Did I deserve to even be on the ice with these guys? Only one way to find out: work my ass off. Which I did, and I performed well in our twice-daily workouts on the ice.

That was an exhilarating feeling. I knew now I had the ability to play. But would I get the chance?

I came back from Montreal and continued to work with Bruce and a couple of other guys on a daily basis. The owner of the local ice rink gave us free time—he knew about me

and wanted to see me realize my dream. I was selling
Medicaid insurance at the time, and my numbers began to
dwindle. My boss told me I needed to make a choice—my
job or my hockey career, if you could call it that. I told him
in no uncertain terms that I was committed to hockey; that
I had to go down this road as far as it would take me.
Surprisingly, he understood and stuck with me.

In late summer 1994 I went to an ECHL tryout camp in
Dublin, Ohio. There I met Storm coach Greg Pahalski. I had
seen him around; he was a former player himself. At the end of
the three-day camp, the ECHL held its draft. I was sitting
there with all the other players, waiting to find out with whom
. . . or even if we would be playing. The coaches and league
officials huddled around a blackboard, with the name of the
teams and the draft choices. The Storm picked fourteenth out
of twenty-one teams. When it was their turn, I heard the
announcement. "With the fourteenth pick, the Storm selects
Todd Crandell."

I was stunned momentarily, and then elated. I walked up,
they put a Storm hat on me, and I shook the hand of the
ECHL commissioner as a photographer snapped our photo.
Even though I would only play part-time, even though my
role would be as a backup, even though it was the ECHL and

not the NHL, I had made it . . . I was now a professional hockey player.

As usual, I went to excess. All that fine hockey gear I'd bought on Larry's Visa card from Perani's? Gone. Now that I was signed with a team, good wasn't good enough; I needed the best. I went out and bought all-new equipment, in the red-and-white team colors of the Storm. The pièce de résistance was my mask. Goalies need a mask, of course, to protect us from the puck; otherwise we'd all end up having faces all battered and stitched up like Frankenstein's monster. But over the years, the mask has also become a personal statement, as well—a kind of vanity plate with eyeholes.

I hired an artist who had painted the masks of some NHL goalies. He painted a white wolf on the front of mine, with fangs—and on the back, my initials. The mask cost me seven hundred dollars; the paint job, four hundred. Now, considering that I was being paid about three hundred and fifty dollars per "call-up"—meaning every time the Storm needed to activate me for practices and games—spending four hundred dollars on the paint job for my mask was an extravagance, to say the least. But whether I was snorting coke or stopping pucks, I wanted to do it with style.

I soon learned, however, that all my fancy new equipment

didn't change the fact that I was now playing in another league—a point that was driven home as soon as I started practicing with the Storm. Some of these kids—most of them were in their late teens and early twenties—would eventually hook on with an NHL team, so they were good, really good. The shots came so much quicker, and harder. It was a challenge and I loved it—and, thanks in part to my conditioning regimen, I was up for it.

My favorite was the rapid-fire drill, the last thing we'd do on the ice before the end of practice. This was designed to sharpen the goalie's reflex times. Two or three players position themselves out on the blue line—sixty feet in front of my goal. One is on the far left, one to the far right, sometimes one in the middle. Then they take turns shooting . . . bam, bam, bam . . . one puck after another, for ten minutes, flying at me. It was up to me to stop 'em all; to stop all these guys who had ganged up on me. I did well at that.

I never bitched about how tough these drills and the practices were. I wanted to work hard. I was the first guy on the ice for practice, and the last to leave. I asked players and coaches if they'd stick around a little late, to keep shooting at me, so I could keep working, keep honing my skills. They didn't seem to mind—neither did most of the players. I think they actually found me kind of intriguing. A five foot, eight-inch, twenty-nine-year-old ex-drug-addict is not your typical roster player. They were curious, asking me about my story. I could see from their expressions and their questions ("Why did you keep doing drugs . . . how did you stop?") that I'd made an impression on them. That was good—almost as good as the news I got from Coach Pahalski the night before our first preseason game, against our ECHL rivals, the Columbus Chill. "I'll be putting you in, third period," he said.

What I had always hoped for was about to come true, but on a scale more suited to real life than dreams. I wouldn't be facing off against Gretzky, but against hungry kids with their own NHL dreams. Here in the ECHL, in an obscure corner of the hockey world, I was about to play my first professional game.

As far as this addict was concerned, it could have been Madison Square Garden in Game 7 of the Stanley Cup finals.

The night before, I called my high school coach Jim Cooper. Back when I had played for him, he would always give me a few good words of advice or encouragement before a game. I asked him if he could do the same now, on the eve of my first appearance in a professional hockey game. He did, and without any rhetorical excess. "Stop the puck," Coop said. "That's your job, Todd. Just stop the puck."

Simple advice. I wish I could say that I followed it.

That evening, I drove into the parking lot of the Toledo Sports Arena for our game against the Chill. I knew this place well. I couldn't help recall that the last time I was at the arena, ten years earlier, I had snorted speed off the floor—the filthy, beer-spattered, walked-over, pissed-on floor—during a Scorpions concert. Now I was here, standing tall, as a professional athlete.

There was a crowd of about three thousand in the arena that night, many Sylvania friends and family members among them. The word had spread that I was going to be making my debut. During warm-ups, I saw out of the corner of my eye my dad taking pictures, Melissa sitting next to him with a big smile. She later told me the whole experience was exciting; she also got her own little payback, something I never knew until years later. At the arena that night, she bumped into an ex-boyfriend of hers. "What are you doing here?" he asked.

"I'm here to see my fiancé," she replied. "He's playing for the Storm." That shut him up good.

I sat and watched the first two periods of the game, tapping my feet, anxious. Then the coach motioned me in and I took the ice. "Now in goal for the Toledo Storm . . . Todd Crandell." This was it, I thought. A dream deferred due to thirteen years of trying to kill myself. But I was alive, and I was on the ice as a professional. Maybe not the way it could have been, but the only way possible now. Amid all the other things I had broken in my life—relationships, promises, hearts—here was one thing, my talent as an athlete, that I had been able to put back together.

I wish I could tell you I put the Chill on ice; shut 'em down, saved the game. I didn't. I had a poor night. The game was tied 5-5 with about a minute left when a guy had a breakaway and was coming toward me—like Gretzky in the dream. In a breakaway, one player from the opposing team comes skating toward the goal at full speed, with the puck in his control and no defensemen around. It's essentially a duel between the guy with the puck trying to score and the goalie trying to stop him. I loved the breakaways; they seemed to distill the essence of what it is to be a goalie into one dramatic, man-to-man confrontation: Stop the puck. Just stop the puck.

In this case, I figured it would be a way to redeem myself,

and have the storybook ending to my first pro game that I hoped for. I was a bit too aggressive. The shooter, who was racing toward me, made a move to his left that I couldn't cover. He slid the puck under my spread-out legs to win the game for the Chill 6-5.

I felt awful, but my teammates were supportive. David Goverde, the first-string goalie for the Storm, a guy who had played with the Los Angeles Kings—Gretzky's team at the time—came up to me. Other goalies understand what it's like to be humiliated in front of thousands of people. "Hey, don't worry about it man," he said. "Happens to all of us."

A couple of days later I went on a road trip with the team to Erie, Pennsylvania. I dressed, but didn't get to play. Then it was on to Huntington, West Virginia, to meet another ECHL rival, the Blizzard. This time I played, and played well. I was calmer now—maybe not having all these people I knew in the stands helped—and it showed. We won, 5-2. I also got booed, the way every rival goalie does, and I loved it. Hearing "Crandell sucks"—even from people who didn't know Crandell—helped motivate me to play harder.

That was it. I dressed for five more games that season, but didn't see any more action. The former LA Kings guy played goal over me—and deservedly so. At the end of the season, another ECHL team offered me a spot on their roster. I probably could have played another season or so. A few more breakaways, a few more "Crandell sucks," a few more saves. I thanked them, but said no. What would have been the beginning of the road for an eighteen-year-old was the end for me, now. I had achieved what I set out to do: proved that I belonged there, proved that I could play, prove that somewhere in my body and soul was a spark that I couldn't douse, despite a decade of trying.

I did keep up my conditioning regimen. I was leaner, more muscular, with greater stamina and energy than at any time in the previous decade. As I ran the streets of Sylvania near our house, I thought about what I wanted to do with my life. I knew I wanted to do something to try to help other addicts, people who were in the same miserable boat as I had been, but wasn't sure how to go about it. That December, I watched the NBC broadcast of the Hawaii Ironman Triathlon. I'd seen this before; it's exercise excess on a scale an addict could truly appreciate. Competitors swam 2.4 miles, rode 112 on a bike, then ran a 26.2-mile marathon, in succession. It was also moving, dramatic, inspiring.

I had an idea.

A professional hockey player at last.

7

Going Long

The most famous and, some say, difficult one-day endurance challenge in the world was sparked by a debate. It was 1977, and a group of runners were gathered for an awards ceremony after a race in Honolulu, the Oahu Perimeter Relay Run. One of the participants, a U.S. Navy captain and runner named John Collins, had just read a magazine article proclaiming Belgian cycling champion Eddy Merckx the fittest athlete in the world. Others disagreed, maintaining that distance runners or swimmers were the best conditioned.

"We got into an argument," Collins recalled years later.

The good-natured debate raged on until Collins had a

brainstorm and, according to his recollections twenty-five years later, leapt on stage and issued a challenge. To settle the question once and for all, he proposed a competition that would tie the three prominent swimming, biking, and running events then held in Hawaii—the 2.4-mile Waikiki Rough-water Swim, the 112-mile Around Oahu Bike Race, and the 26.2-mile Honolulu Marathon—into one mega-race. "I said, 'the gun will go off about 7 A.M., the clock will keep running and whoever finishes first, we'll call the Ironman,'" Collins said.

The following February, 1978, fifteen competitors, including Collins, competed in the first Ironman triathlon. Held on Oahu, the course followed the routes of the other three existing events. Twelve of the fifteen, including Collins, went the entire distance. The winner, Gordon Haller (described as a "taxicab driver and fitness enthusiast"), won that first race in a time of 11 hours, 46 minutes, 56 seconds. Collins himself finished in a little under seventeen hours.

At the start of that first race, each of the competitors received a handout with the course descriptions and some rules for the fledgling competition. On the last page was scribbled this call to action: "Swim 2.4 miles! Bike 112 miles! Run 26.2 miles! Brag for the rest of your life!"

Eventually thousands of people would come to Hawaii in an attempt to earn these bragging rights.

The new competition caught on fast, helped in part by the media, always attracted to stories about people doing crazy or extreme things: A feature in *Sports Illustrated* led to an ABC telecast in 1980. This generated interest in the Ironman around the world and—helped by inspiring televised images of athletes crawling across the finish line—eventually led to a worldwide series of twenty-six full- or half-distance Ironman races from Lake Placid, New York, to Lanzarote in the Canary Islands. These events have soared in popularity to the point that registration now fills up a year in advance. Meanwhile, the Hawaii event, now known as the Ironman Triathlon World Championship, attracts an annual field of about seventeen hundred participants, including many pro-fessionals (a concept unheard of in 1978), not to mention a television audience of millions who watch the annual Emmy-winning broadcast of the race, now carried by NBC.

At age twenty-one I had sat enthralled in front of the TV in my apartment in Sylvania, watching the Ironman telecast from far-off, exotic Hawaii, thinking what a great achieve-ment it must be to finish. It seemed to me that this was the ultimate individual test in sports. I wondered whether I could do it. The fact that I was smoking crack while I was watching would suggest the answer was no. But that was then. By 1998 I had been sober five years.

I was done with the Storm and needed something else, a new sport or physical activity, not only to keep me fit but also to help fill the hours after work. "Idle hands are the devil's playthings" is a slogan that applies well to ex-addicts. We need to keep busy. We need to channel our addictive energies into something positive, and away from the craving that still gnaws at us.

With my hockey career over, triathlon seemed like that positive outlet to me. As was the case with my spending spree on goalie equipment when I joined the Storm, I wanted only the best for my new sport. I purchased a two-thousand-dollar Cannondale bicycle and on a crisp afternoon in April 1998 went out for a ride in the neighborhood. I was excited—my first step toward being an Ironman, I thought.

It was great, until I was hit head-on by a car.

The car had turned suddenly in front of me; I plowed into the front right side of the grille, went rolling over the hood, and landed in the street on my keister. "Where did you come from?" I remember the driver asking as she rushed over to me. "Mommy," said her little daughter, who had run up beside her, "he was right in front of you." Meanwhile, her husband, who was not driving, looked frightened. "Don't move," he said. "Your leg is bleeding really badly . . . it doesn't look good."

Great, I thought, I survive professional hockey to get a crippling injury riding my bike two blocks from home. But then I realized that the husband was looking at the big dragon tattoo I have on my left calf. "I'm not hurt," I said. "But my bike probably is."

It was smashed up. And while they were honest enough to pay for the cost of a new one, the accident spelled the end of training for that year.

My triathlon career, take two: In February 1999 I resolved to try again. This time I decided to focus on the swim. I went to our local Vic Tanny's, which had a pool about fifteen or twenty yards long. I jumped in one end, started thrashing away, and by the time I got to the other end, I thought I was going to pass out. My pursuit of the great distances of the Ironman was going nowhere. How the hell was I going to swim a mile, much less 2.4 in an Ironman, if I could barely make twenty yards?

But I was as determined to do a triathlon as I had once been to get myself wasted. I decided to apply a lesson I had learned from my recovery: I got help. I went to a former neighbor of mine, an outstanding swimmer, and asked him to show me how to swim. The guy was flabbergasted at first. Last time he had seen me, I was in the full throes of my addiction. In fact, he told me that was one of the reasons he had moved. "I couldn't stand watching you kill yourself," he said.

Now that I had decided to stay alive, he was eager to assist. He accompanied me back to Vic Tanny's. We hopped in the pool together. He showed me proper technique and breathing. He made me realize that brute strength and will were not the answer here. Slowly but surely, I began feeling more comfortable and control in the water. Meanwhile, I was managing to ride my bike without colliding with any cars and was getting up at 5 A.M. to do my runs. They seemed very long at the time—three or four miles.

I had a local Sylvania triathlon in mind as my goal, and I was psyched. I became consumed with the sport, learning as much as I could about it. While perusing the web one night, I came across some startling information. I had known about the Ironman in Hawaii, of course. But you had to qualify to get into that race. What I didn't know, and found out that night, was that there were other Ironman distance triathlons —including one in my old stomping grounds, Florida.

"This is it!" I told Melissa that night. "I am doing this!"

I signed up for Ironman Florida—which was being held in November 1999, about eight months away. It cost me three hundred and fifty dollars for the privilege of going to kill myself. For good measure, I also signed up for Ironman California. I could barely swim, my longest runs were about one-fifth of the marathon distance, and I had already committed to doing two Ironman triathlons. Melissa was supportive—but not so my dad. "An Ironman?" he said when I dropped by his office to tell him. "You don't even know how to swim!"

As always, being told I couldn't do something made me more determined to proceed. I got a program from a triathlon magazine and started planning. I didn't always follow it, as my enthusiasm ran away with me. In one case, literally so: At a point when I was supposed to be covering eight to ten miles in running, I went out and ran seventeen miles in the rain just to see if I could do it. The soreness in my legs that hampered my training for the next week taught me an important lesson: Progress in triathlon is incremental. Again, I tried to equate it with recovery. As the old cliché goes, I was trying to stay sober "one day at a time." In my training, I was doing something similar—taking small, daily steps toward my ultimate goal.

A shorter race was a first step. I found a so-called sprint-distance tri in the Wendy's Sprint Triathlon in Columbus, Ohio, in June 1999. These are entry-level tris, generally consisting of a half-mile swim, twelve-mile bike, and a 5K (3.1-mile) run. I was eager and excited, but not nervous. Considering my sporadic training, I felt good, finishing in about one hour and thirty minutes.

I hasten to point out that the top sprint triathletes finish in less than sixty minutes. My finish time that day led me to another realization. Unlike hockey, triathlon didn't come so easily to me. I don't remember stumbling and falling on the ice as I was learning to skate. I don't recall a time when a hockey stick in my hands didn't feel as comfortable as a pair of gloves. I rarely had to summon a great deal of effort to react to shots—it just seemed to happen.

In triathlon, it was different. My body, well sized to protect a net and present a small target in a rink, was not as well proportioned for endurance activities. I didn't have the shoulders of the swimmer, the legs of the bicyclist, the lungs of the marathon runner. Even when it went relatively well, as it did in that first sprint tri, it was always a struggle at some level, and after that first race—as I watched guys twice my age and many women leave me in the dust—I realized I would probably never be more than average in triathlon.

At first I brooded about this, but not for long. I decided that I was more interested in being involved with this fascinating sport than being really proficient at it. Would it be fun to be world-class in triathlon? Sure, but I'd had a fleeting taste of being a pro in another sport, so being "the best" wasn't quite as important to me here. Besides, I knew I never would be.

Still, I was pumped. Like many people who rush pell-mell into endurance sports, I overtrained, and the results were predictable: Near the end of summer I started having some bad knee pains. My reaction was equally foreseeable: I tried to train through it. The pain got worse, and I finally had to see an orthopedist. He told me I had three tears in the meniscus of my left knee. I gobbled anti-inflammatories and moved on with my training, except I could only bike and swim, not run.

On Halloween day 1999 we went trick-or-treating with our now one-year-old daughter Skylar. After she'd collected her fill of candy, we dropped her off with my parents, and Melissa and I headed down to Florida for what I'm sure to many in Sylvania seemed like the latest bizarre Crandell adventure. Our Honda Odyssey minivan was packed to the gills—although I couldn't help notice that unlike my last big trip down here, in 1987, the trunk was filled not with cases of beer, booze and carefully wrapped bags of cocaine and weed, but rather with all my triathlon gear: my racing bike and helmet, my wetsuit, my running shoes and so forth.

During my training I had met another triathlete from Sylvania, Scott Horns, who had signed up for Florida as well. This would be his third Ironman—he was actually good at this—and he would later become my coach. Melissa and I invited him to drive down with us.

The three of us drove through the night, about twenty hours, arriving in Panama City, Florida, on a drizzly overcast November morning. I brought my video camera along to soak up every minute of the Ironman experience, from my number pickup (I was number 636) to unpacking in our hotel room. There I am on video, spending hundreds of dollars on every piece of merchandise with the Ironman logo on it I could find. By the end of the trip, I would have Ironman shorts, shirts, watches . . . and I would even have an Ironman arm: I had scheduled an appointment with a friend, tattoo artist "Monk" Taylor in Toledo to have the logo emblazoned on my right arm, the day after I returned . . . confident that

I would finish.

Some doubts crossed my mind, the second day there, when I went out for a swim in the ocean and found myself flailing around in huge waves. The weather was not good. My swim cap got knocked off, and they had the red flags out. Here I was, a guy from landlocked Ohio, faced with an angry Gulf of Mexico. I remember asking Scott, "Are we going to have to swim in this?" He said, "It's not so bad once you get past the first couple of swells." *Either that,* I thought, *or you drown.*

There was some good news. I was running pain-free—thanks to drugs, although not illegal ones, this time. I had cortisone shot in my knee before we left, and the day before the race, I went for a short jog. Felt great. "Hey," I thought to myself. "I can run the marathon part of this pain free."

It was just one of many wrong assumptions I made that weekend.

On race day I arose at 4 A.M. My breakfast was a smoothie of bananas, protein powder, carrots, strawberries, pineapple juice, and yogurt—blended together as quietly as I could to keep from waking Melissa. I couldn't believe I was about to do this.

Packing for the Ironman is nearly as much of a challenge

as training for it. I must have had a dozen bags of various sizes lying around the hotel, filled with all the stuff I needed: wetsuit, swim goggles and cap, timing chip, racing bike, towel, bike glasses, helmet, race number, bike shoes, bike top, bike lock, tire pump, extra bike tools, running shoes, running glasses, energy gels, Gatorade, bananas, PowerBars, salt tablets, and of course, my Mötley Crüe CD to listen to and get pumped up.

Walking out to the van, looking like a triathlon pack mule, I was surprised to see a big poster stuck into the windshield of the van. The exhortation GO TODD! was written on it in big black letters. Melissa had created this after I fell asleep the previous evening. Again, I thanked my lucky stars that she had come along for the ride to Florida, and to wherever else life was going to take us.

I got down to the race site and started to walk toward the "body marking" area. Sounds grim, but it's actually a line where volunteers use a special black marker to write your race number on your arm and leg. "I guess this is in case you drown, they can identify the body," I joked to a guy standing next to me. He didn't laugh.

You could hear the announcer welcoming everyone and soft music playing in the background. It was still dark, and a sense of quiet tension, balled-up anxiety was almost palpable. Quite obviously, everybody here was as nervous as I was. But there were still preparations to be made. With my race number 636 barely legible next to my various tattoos, I walked over to the bike station inside the transition area. This is the central staging area in a triathlon: the point along the route where the athletes change ("transition") from swimming to bicycling, and later from bicycling to running. Part changing room, part open-air equipment locker, it's the focal point of the event. Races are won and lost by how much time a triathlete takes in this area. Imagine losing a race because you never learned how to tie your shoes quickly enough.

Fast transitions . . . heck, fast anything . . . were not my concern this morning. My goal was to finish and live to tell the tale. I needed to do everything methodically, carefully, within my comfort level. That included getting my equipment ready. I put my sixteen-ounce water bottles, filled with Gatorade, onto the holders mounted on the back of my bike seat, wiped the morning mist off the bike seat, pumped my tires one last time, placed my biking shoes on the toe clips and stuffed my energy bars and gels into the little box that fastens onto the cross-tube of the bike. Around me, hundreds of others were doing the same. Some of these people looked like their skin had been glazed on over their muscles with a paintbrush, they were so lean, hard, and fit. I felt grateful, honored, and lucky to be here. While I couldn't compare myself to the hard bodies around me, I sure felt closer to them than to the person I had once been here: the guy who had prowled these beaches in search of drugs, or spent days passed out on the beach.

After finishing with my bike I stripped out of my dry clothes, put on my wetsuit, grabbed my swim cap and goggles, and headed out of the transition area to find my wife Melissa. We walked together down to the swim start just as the sun was coming up. A vivid orange sun was rising over what appeared to be a mercifully calm ocean; the rays illuminated the white sandy beaches.

The swim course was marked with large orange buoys that stretched out so far, you could hardly seem them. It was a 1.2-mile swim course that we would do twice. That meant seventeen hundred people crammed into a relatively narrow swim lane. Mass swim starts are always dicey in triathlons. There's a lot of heads being kicked and people swimming over one another. As the music got louder and more uptempo, I began to get nervous. Could I go the distance? Had I trained properly? What if somebody kicked me in the face in the first hundred yards and that was the end of my race?

Boom! The cannon fired, the race was on, and I remember thinking there was no turning back now; *just do it.*

The first few hundred yards were intense, with arms and legs flying everywhere—triathletes often describe it as feeling as if they're in a washing machine—but eventually the crowds opened up. While the taste of salt water was foreign to my Midwest mouth, I soon found my space and settled into a groove—two strokes, breathe out of the left side, slow flutter kick. I puttered along like this back and forth for the two 1.2-mile loops, finishing the swim in 1 hour, 11 minutes (by comparison, the first athletes out of the water in an Ironman are usually done in forty-eight to fifty-two minutes).

Out of the water we came, up on the beach for fifty or sixty yards, through a timing chute and into the transition area. I grabbed my bike clothes off the rack and went into the changing tent. I'd never before seen so many people in a state of undress. I stripped off my wetsuit, pulled up my biking shorts, put on my jersey and helmet, raced out of the tent to my bike, and started on my 112-mile journey in the Florida sunshine. This is the single longest stretch of the Ironman, and I had to settle in for what would amount to over six hours of cycling. The first four hours flew by. The course was flat, the weather warm and sunny. *This is great,* I remember thinking as we blasted up Highway 79. *Maybe this isn't going to be as bad as everybody says.*

That changed after about eighty miles. I began to feel tired, I began to feel the heat, I began to feel cramps in my legs. I began to feel, as some of the old-timers say, as if the bear had jumped on my back. Now my glycogen stores were beginning to get depleted despite my frantic attempts to keep the tank reasonably full with Gatorade, bananas, and Power-Bars. Now, I just couldn't wait to get off the damn bike. Thirty miles left: I tried to visualize crossing the finish line— still over fifty-seven miles away, which in retrospect was not such a good thing to focus on—as I continued struggling through the last miles of the bike leg.

Finally, after 6 hours, 11 minutes, I pulled into the transition area. I had now been moving continually for nearly eight hours—a full day's work—and I still had a marathon to run.

My legs stiff from riding for all that time, I gingerly climbed off the bike, handed it to a volunteer who racked it for me, and then jogged back to the changing room to lace on my running shoes. As I shuffled out of the transition area, I spotted Melissa, waving and cheering for me. That pumped me up for the first couple of miles of the run. At about mile 4, however, my knee pain returned as the cortisone shot wore off. It got worse and worse. Then my lower back began to ache, reducing me to a walk. I started to second guess this whole idea. What was I doing here? I didn't need to be doing this to prove anything or even to stay in shape. This was beyond fitness . . . this was madness!

I heard cheering. I looked up and saw two attractive young girls standing on the balcony of their condo, looking down at us. "I'm dying!" I called out. "Give me some inspiration!" One of them pulled up her shirt and shook her ample breasts. I couldn't believe it. A guy behind me started laughing. "That was awesome!" he said. "Thanks!"

The light—or was it lewd?—moment relaxed me enough to take my mind off the pain. I was able to start running for a while, before being reduced again to a walk. That's the way it went for the next fifteen miles, as I settled into a Death-March-like ratio: a slow, cramped jog for five minutes, then a staggering walk for ten minutes. At mile twenty—6.2 miles to go in the entire race—I saw Melissa. "What the hell is taking you so long?" she called out. This has become her signature line at every race I've done since, and we laugh about it. That day in Florida, however, she was genuinely concerned. She came out on the course and jogged with me for a bit as

I struggled on, but I told her to go back to the finish and wait. "I'll be there soon," I said.

There is a cutoff time in the Ironman: after seventeen hours, you are not an official finisher. I was determined to make it across the line before then, and as I got closer and closer, I realized I would make it. At mile twenty-five, I could hear cheering in the distance and the announcer's voice over the loudspeaker announcing the names of finishers as they crossed the line. I started to run again. It was now about 8:30 P.M. I had been racing since 7:00 A.M. and on my feet since 2:30 in the afternoon—a horribly slow, painful marathon. The finish area was brightly lit, and I squinted in the flood-lights after being in darkness for so long. Race organizers had laid out a carpet for the last twenty-five yards, and these were twenty-five of the best yards of my life. I was floating at this point—surrounded by people wildly screaming, music, a wall of noise erected in what had been a desert of silence and pain. And then an almost surreal moment: a voice calling my name. It was the race announcer, and he was saying something as if out of a dream: A dream now come true. "Todd Crandell," I heard, as I staggered across the line in 14 hours, 12 minutes, and right into Melissa's arms. "*You* are an Ironman."

8

Racing for Recovery

My Florida experience hooked me on Ironman. I began to embrace a new lifestyle—I was not only sober, but also fit. My days now began to revolve around swim practices in the morning, runs at lunchtime, bike rides after work or on the weekends. My efforts began to pay off: I got lighter and leaner. I was still no stud, at least compared with the top triathletes, but I certainly wasn't a spud, either. My times got better; I felt more comfortable in each of the three disciplines. And then, just before I left Sylvania for my fourth Ironman, in Auckland, New Zealand, something happened that would change my life, again.

I made a telephone call.

It was to the *Toledo Blade*, our major local newspaper. At the suggestion of some of my friends, who thought what I was doing in triathlon was pretty cool (especially considering where I'd come from), I called the Sports Department and spoke to a reporter who answered the phone. As a salesman, I knew a little bit about how to make cold calls, and I cut right to the chase, laying out what has now become my standard *this is my life in sixty seconds* pitch to the media.

"Hi, my name is Todd Crandell," I said. "I have a story for you that deals with thirteen years of cocaine, crack, and alcohol abuse, which resulted in three drunk driving charges, ruining a promising hockey career, and living in my car . . . to now twelve years of sobriety and doing the Ironman triathlon four times." All in one breath.

"Interesting," said the writer. "Where can we meet?"

I met John Wagner, sportswriter for the *Blade*, at the local Olive Garden restaurant, and he proceeded to ask me a whole lot of questions. He also established a ground rule for the interview; a good one, I thought, that applies for me to this day. "I am not going to cover this story unless you promise to tell it all and tell it honestly," he said.

I appreciated that. All the lying during my drug days had changed something in me. Now all I wanted to do was tell the truth, and nothing but. "Absolutely," I said. "I'll tell you everything. I won't spare any of the gory details."

So I began to talk, the same way I've been talking to you through the pages of this book. As I got into some of the details of my debauchery, I noticed that Wagner had a blank look on his face. Finally I asked him if anything was wrong. "Are you kidding me with this?" he asked. "Is this for real?" When I assured him it was, I could tell he was pleased. He knew this was going to be a great story. Wagner told me that we'd finish up when I returned from New Zealand.

After I got back, we met again. A *Blade* photographer came to my house and took pictures of me running and riding on the stationary bike in my garage, and holding up my New Zealand finishing medal. Wagner's profile on me appeared in the *Blade* on April 14, 2001—the day before my eighth year of sobriety. It ran on page one of the *Blade*'s Sports section, right next to early-season baseball stories about the Detroit Tigers, the Cleveland Indians, and our local minor-league franchise, the Toledo Mud Hens. But for that day, Crandell left the Mud Hens in the dust. My story (okay, it must have been a slow news day) was the most prominent one on the page.

Wagner did a fine job, drawing the contrast of my life then

and now. "Today's Crandell is a triathlete who spends roughly twenty hours a week working out, preparing to compete in Ironman triathlons," he wrote. "The 'old' Crandell wasn't an athlete—unless drug and alcohol abuse constitutes a sport. If it does, at one time Crandell was an Olympic champion in that."

"This is cool," I thought, as I climbed on my bike that morning for a fifty-mile ride.

"Hey, Todd, nice story in the paper," said my neighbor as I pulled out of the driveway. I thanked him and pedaled away, thinking how nice it was to be a star on the block—at least for the day.

When I got back, though, Melissa was waiting for me outside. I thought something was wrong. "Todd," she said. "The phone has been ringing off the hook from that story." She wasn't kidding. Over the next few days, it seemed as if everyone I had ever met in my life was calling me: former teachers, teammates, people I did drugs with, cops who had arrested me for doing drugs. I was stunned. This was more than just *Hey, I saw your picture in the paper.* That's when it first occurred to me that what I had been through in my life—and the fact that I had survived and move on to a much better place—could really inspire others. I began to think that instead of doing these Ironman triathlons just to feel good about myself, I could use them to help people who had been in the same boat I once was. This was a moment of self-awareness almost as critical as the day I put down the beer at Granny's house.

The *Blade* story was the catalyst for me to get this story out and help people change their lives.

I wanted to achieve two things: First, to prevent substance abuse among kids, and second, to show the person who is battling addictions that recovery is possible. Of course, there are lots of organizations that have been successful in doing just that. I myself had gone to AA, and benefited from the experience.

Still, from the calls I was getting—and soon, it wasn't people I knew but mostly individuals with friends or loved ones battling substance abuse—I began to see that part of what made my approach to recovery different was the fact that I was not a psychologist, an educator, a Bible-thumper, or a policy maker. I was an ex-addict. That gave me a lot more credibility with addicts who were still using, or fighting hard not to. I knew what it was like. I knew what they were going through. And I could offer them an alternative. I had channeled my addictive energy into a more positive vein—into physical activity, exercise and sport.

As I thought about this, I began to imagine how I could

reach more people, not just the ones who called me after reading the *Blade* article. Maybe some kind of group would be the way to go: an organized, not-for-profit foundation that would provide me with a platform for getting the word out. I thought about what Race for the Cure had done for breast cancer awareness and research. I admire that organization tremendously. They started small and local, but grew to become one of the most successful fund-raisers in the country. That also sparked the idea for a name. Instead of a Race for the Cure, we would be about Racing for Recovery. One night, I cobbled together a mission statement:

The mission of Racing for Recovery is to prevent all forms of substance abuse and to provide positive alternatives for those currently battling addictions by encouraging a lifestyle of fitness and health through 5K run/walk events across the nation.

I was pumped, psyched, and ready to go. As so often happened in my life, however, not everybody shared my enthusiasm. I called my attorney to tell him about my idea of establishing a not-for-profit organization. "It'll never work," he said. This was the same response I've gotten for many years: "You'll never get off drugs," "You'll never amount to anything," "How can you do an Ironman? You can't even swim." His reaction disappointed me, but also fueled me to make this thing work.

Following the Race for the Cure model, we decided to develop a series of 5K road races. That's 3.1 miles—a distance that most people can run or walk, with just a little training. We targeted October 26, 2002, as the date for our first one in Sylvania.

That event was the culmination of a full year of work. Organizing a road race is a lot harder than running in one. There are permits that need to be acquired, insurance policies that need to be drawn up. The police need to be involved, neighbors need to be notified, sponsors have to be found. And, perhaps most importantly, the community needs to be behind it. Getting Sylvania to support the drug abuse prevention race organized by the guy who was once the town's most prominent drug abuser became the main focus of my activities.

I contacted everyone I knew. I hung posters everywhere in town, put flyers in truck stops and on windshields, handed them out to strangers. When I went to a drive-through to pick up dinner for Melissa and our two children, Skylar and Konor, I would hand the attendant a flyer. I'd leave stacks of them in gas stations, grocery stores, at the old hockey rink. I got a lot of, "Well, I'm not a runner." I explained that it wasn't just for runners; it was an event to bring the community together and fight substance abuse.

I got some raised eyebrows from people who remembered me from the old days. I think some of them glanced at the flyer and thought I was really holding this race in order to raise money to *buy* drugs. But I also got a lot of encouragement from people who were moved by what I had done and what I was trying to do.

A few weeks before the race, the local drug rehab clinic, Compass, invited me in to talk about myself and the race. With the addicts, my message was *If I can do it, so can you.* With young people—obviously a key target audience for us—it was *Don't do as I've done . . . at least over the first part of my life.* And, of course, I invited them all to get involved in the race, in one way or another.

My old school, Northview, declined my offer to talk to their students. But Whitmer High in Toledo accepted. That was ironic. This was our big rival, the same school whose students had once chanted "Crandell sucks" during our hockey games. Now they were letting Crandell in, to deliver what they realized was an important message.

I spoke to an assembly of students, grades nine through twelve, expecting a lot of blank stares or giggling or inattentiveness. But they sat mesmerized as I told them the stuff I'd done when I was their age, or not much older. The race part of my talk, I wasn't sure—running three miles was probably not their idea of what to do on a Saturday morning. Still, I must have made an impact. As with the *Blade* story, the reactions from the kids were even more heartfelt and powerful than I had expected. Within a day or two of speaking at Whitmer, I began to receive letters from the students—many of them, I later learned, unprompted by teachers. Here are two that I kept:

Dear Mr. Crandell,

Thank you for coming and talking to my class and telling us your story. It helped me better understand what drugs can do to good people. The story you told really made me think about the people I am close to and what could happen to some of them if they're not careful with their choices. But most importantly you taught me how I can help them without trying to control them and what they do. I just wanted to say thank you for everything. The picture that you wrote a message on for me now hangs on my wall to remind me that I'm on the right track and to never let anyone try to tell me otherwise. Even though you may not remember me thank you for everything.

Sincerely,

Cristal

Dear Todd Crandell,

Thank you for coming to Whitmer to speak to our class about your experiences with drug and alcohol addictions. I think its incredible what you have overcome and it is really great how you've turned your life around. I also think Racing for Recovery is great and I hope to participate in this year's run/walk. I never realized how quickly someone could become addicted until after hearing your story. I think it is very upsetting that some people may never get rid of their addictions or get help with their addictions, but it feels really good to know that someone is making an attempt to help those people. Your story has also encouraged me to stay drug and alcohol free. Thanks again.

Sincerely,

Ashley

As far as I was concerned, the race was already a success. But of course, we also needed more tangible results—like participants and spectators. As the days ticked down to October 26, I got more and more nervous. What if we held a race and nobody came? How ridiculous would that look? *Racing for Recovery, born and died on the same day.*

The night before the event, the race management company I had hired to do the timing arrived in town and set up their trailer on the campus of Lourdes College, where I had graduated with a degree in business. That evening Melissa, my kids, some friends, and I were at my house, filling the race bags—the package that each registered runner would receive, including their race chip, number, and the fancy long-sleeved race T-shirts, featuring the new Racing for Recovery logo (a local design firm did it for me pro bono, and won an award for it). We were up most of the night, laughing, giddy, excited about the whole thing.

Then it started to rain. The mood changed abruptly. "We're sunk," I said, gazing glumly out the window.

I hardly slept that night, and arrived at the college by 5:30 A.M. The drizzle continued as I paced nervously around the empty staging area. I remember seeing the first people arrive; I thought maybe they were students at Lourdes, showing up for some early-morning Saturday class or to go to the library. But no, it was some of the kids from Whitmer High! I practically hugged them, I was so excited to see them. Then some old friends arrived; then family members, community people, runners alone and in small groups. By the time the race started, the Lourdes College parking lot was packed. There were hundreds of people there—some running, some walking, some cheering, some volunteering.

Before the start, I got up on top of the race trailer and addressed the crowd. I saw Melissa and the kids looking up at me ("Hi Daddy!" called Skylar). My dad and stepmom were there, Granny was there. Coach Cooper was there, ready to run the 5K, in fact. I saw some of my old hockey teammates and former drinking buddies. It took everything I had to not break down and cry, I was so moved by the turnout.

A total of 202 people finished the race; another hundred came to watch or help out at the event. The runners came from as far away as New York. The out-of-towners had seen a small article on me in *Triathlete* magazine. They were inspired and decided to show up. I was flabbergasted.

At 9 A.M. I fired the starting gun, then jumped into the pack as it thundered by. No way was I going to miss running in my race! I made a point to help pace a couple of the kids. We talked a little during the race. People called out as I passed, "Todd, this is great! What a wonderful day!"

It really was.

We lost money on that first 5K. But we gained something more important. The event made Racing for Recovery a reality. In the next couple of years, we would develop five in-person support group meetings and one online meeting; we'd begin to do more and more speaking engagements, not only in Ohio, but around the country as well. We formed a Team Racing for Recovery, which now has about one hundred members from around the world, many of them recovered substance abusers, or people with friends and family who have battled addiction. Team members function basically as ambassadors for our program, sharing their experiences and how the organization and its events have helped them.

Speaking of events, we added 5Ks in California, New York, and Alabama. In June, 2005, we held our first Half Ironman Triathlon in Sylvania, the logistics of which made the first 5K seem easy. Meanwhile, that race keeps rolling on. By 2004, the Racing for Recovery 5K in Sylvania had doubled in size, to over four hundred participants, making us one of the largest road races in the Toledo area.

There's a lingering, bittersweet memory from that first 5K in 2002 that shows the reality of recovery and reminds me on a daily basis of the importance of what we try to do.

The week before, I had spoken at a local youth detention facility. One of the kids, named Frank, was sixteen at the time, and had already been arrested for a crime involving drugs. He came up to me after my talk, and we chatted for a while about my experiences and his. He really wanted to run the race. I wasn't sure I would see him that day, but sure enough, Frank arrived at Lourdes that morning. He had begged the program director to grant him a one-day release to participate. He ran the 5K and spent some time with us afterward.

In late 2005, three years since I'd seen him, I got a call from Frank. I'd like to tell you that he is now a doctor or lawyer. He's not. He's incarcerated. But in lieu of prison, he chose the recovery treatment center, which is essentially jail for addicts. He called me for help. He remembered my story; he remembered the race. And he said that Racing for Recovery made the biggest impact of all the various rehab programs he'd been through.

This is the reality of addiction: Recovery is not for those who need it, it's for those who want it. All the 5Ks in the world, all the best efforts of Racing for Recovery or any other substance treatment program, cannot change that fact. One of the things we can do, however, is to let those who struggle with addiction know that when they are ready, when they genuinely do want to recover, we are there for them.

I'm still here for you, Frank.

9

Ironman Korea, Ironman Forever

Addiction is a great equalizer.

Every Thursday night, as we gather around the conference table in the basement of the local church for our Racing for Recovery meetings, I am amazed at the diversity.

I see buzz cuts and I see gray hair. I see hip-hop kids and I see guys who look like my accountant. I see nose rings and tattoos, and I see high heels and jackets-and-ties. No class, no race, no gender is excluded. High school dropouts are accepted into our club—and so are PhDs. Liberals, conservatives, Republicans and Democrats; no matter which party is in power, our powerlessness over drugs and alcohol binds us.

The difference is that some have managed to find a way to

elude its grasp. The purpose of our meetings is to help those who haven't. The difference between our support group meetings and others is that we invite both the addict and his or her family to participate together—or on their own, as is the case with many family members, who have found in our Racing for Recovery support meetings a place to talk about and share the challenges they face. Those challenges are enormous, as was evidenced in a recent but not atypical meeting.

As usual, I start the meeting at 7 P.M., asking everyone to introduce themselves. There are some familiar faces here tonight, and some new ones. Donna is new.

"I'm not sure what to say," she says when it's her turn.

"Just say something like this," I suggest. " 'I'm Todd, I'm here because I need to be here, I want to be here, I'm glad to be here.' "

"I need to be here," says Donna, in a meek voice. "I want to be here."

"I'm Jeff," says the guy next to her, reassuringly. "I've been sober for a year and I think we can all help each other."

"I'm so angry, I don't want to talk," says C. J.

We know C. J. She's been here before. Her adult son is a drug addict, and she can't seem to admit it. Like most parents who love their kids, she keeps giving him second chances.

She has become an enabler, which is one of those cute pop psychology labels, but in the world of addiction it really means something. Last week she told us that she had kicked her son out of her house. Now, she admits, he's back home.

"Why did you let him back in?" I ask as gently as I can.

"Because I love him," she answers, her angry eyes brimming with tears as she finally looks me in the face. "I love him . . ." She stops. Her voice drops as she lowers her head. ". . . and I hate him. At the same time."

There's a silence. Finally, a woman wearing the colors of a motorcycle club, who has accompanied her massive husband with tattoos and ponytail, turns and speaks to C. J. "Listen to me," she says. "I lied, cheated, and stole when I was using. I got away with everything, and then I almost lost everything. You've got to love somebody enough to let them hate you."

"He said he needed the money until Monday," says C. J., now crying. "I'm sorry . . . ," she adds apologetically, between sobs.

"There's nothing to be embarrassed about," I tell her. "We understand, because we're exactly the same people as your son. We used drugs, we used alcohol, and we hurt a lot of people along the way until we were able to get control of our addiction. It's not fair for you to suffer because of us."

An older woman, who is here with her bespectacled, CEO-looking husband—they appear as if they could have been looking for the local country club and stumbled in by accident—turns to C. J.

"We have four sons," she says. "Two of them are addicts."

C. J. shakes her head in sympathetic disbelief. Then her anguish turns to anger. "Why are drugs so prevalent in our society?" she asks out loud. "What's going on? It's all around us, and it's just getting worse! These kids think it's cool."

I politely disagree. Having spoken to enough schools, I think I have a sense of what kids think about this. "None of us want to grow up to be addicts," I tell her. "But some of us have this makeup. Our brains are wired a little differently. We make bad decisions. There's nothing cool about it."

The father of the four sons speaks up. "My son stole five hundred dollars from my wallet," he says. "Should I call the cops?"

"It's a robbery," I reply. "It's tough, I know, but you have got to make a stand."

"But I don't want my son to go to jail."

"I'm not a police officer," I say. "But I've been arrested by enough of 'em to know something about how this works. If it's his first offense, he'll get probation. The bottom line"—I'm speaking to him but glancing over to C.J., who is still sitting with her head bowed—"is that whatever's going on doesn't seem to be working. You've got to change your approach."

Suddenly it is 8 P.M. "The meeting is sixty minutes long," I say. "But if you want to stay for a while longer and talk, we can."

Nobody moves.

It was a good meeting, I tell myself later as I walk out of the church. I think with pride about Jeff and how well he's doing; I'm impressed and curious about the biker woman and her husband; I'm worried about C. J. They're all on my mind as I maneuver out of the parking lot for the short drive home.

They're still on my mind as I pedal down a highway on the other side of the world, months later. The meetings, the foundation, the people, the message. They're never far from my thoughts, even when I'm in some far-off place, like Korea, the site of my tenth Ironman, in August 2005.

We are on Jeju, a 712-square mile tropical island located about sixty miles southwest of the Korean mainland. I'm tired and wired at the same time. I haven't been able to sleep because of the time difference and the nineteen-hour flight. Unsure of the effects the local cuisine might have on my stomach, I'm living on MET-Rx shake packages, tuna fish, bananas, and peanut butter. I'm also quite frankly not sure exactly why I'm here. Although race organizers had eagerly welcomed my presence at Ironman Korea, their country has virtually no substance abuse—my message of sobriety is lost on a sober people. On top of it all, I'm twisted inside with the usual Ironman jitters.

Only now, as we roll up and down a hilly highway along the Yellow Sea, can I begin to relax. I'm wondering how Jeremy's doing. He's one of the only other Americans in this field of nearly eight hundred, mostly Japanese, Koreans, and Australians. Jeremy is nineteen; it's his first Ironman and I bumped into him at the beach two days before the race. Jeremy, a Texan, knew about me—he'd seen me interviewed on television in Lubbock when I was there for a Half Ironman. He had no place to stay, no race plan, no nothing. I let him stay with me, and helped get him through the long, pre-race checklist of things you need to attend to before an Ironman: pumping up the tires, packing your salt tablets, getting your gear bags ready; all the little details I had learned since my first Ironman in Florida.

Helping Jeremy get ready for his race also took the focus off my own pre-race anxieties. But as soon as we hit the water, all the tension dissipated. The water was warm and flat—one of the most enjoyable swims I've ever had in an Ironman. The bike, advertised as a flat course, was anything but. Still, I was now in a rhythm and as I watched the lush, tropical scenery of Jeju—a popular honeymoon spot for Korean newlyweds—I couldn't help think of just how far away I was from Sylvania, from Melissa and the kids, and also from my other life.

It was now twelve years since I had put down that last drink at Granny's. My life was transformed. And although I had found sobriety, I still had not found peace. Who has? Instead of worrying about where to get my next gram of coke, I'm worrying now about balancing the books for our foundation. When I was an addict, I had few responsibilities (and yet still managed to behave irresponsibly). Now five people—Melissa and our four children: Skylar, Konor, Madison, and Mason—depend on me. It's as stressful for me as it is for every other adult in early-twenty-first-century America. But knowing that I don't have to reach for a drink to deal with it makes me proud. As does the fact that my foundation is growing; that my inbox is filled almost every day with e-mails from people who have been impacted by Racing for Recovery; that I'm reaching new audiences all the time, from the presentation I gave on recovery alternatives to the Ohio State Supreme Court to the talk I gave to the PTA at my daughter Skylar's elementary school.

At every hill, as my weary calves pump away at the pedals, I think of what one of our team members, a former addict from Toronto, told me. "You're doing this for the addict that didn't make it last night and won't make it today," he said.

It's true—but I also like to think I'm doing it to help some who *will* make it; to inspire them to take the fork on the road that is always available to them when they're ready. Some will never be. Many others are. It's a question of time, just like the endless hours of the Ironman.

At the bike-run transition, friendly people applaud and encourage me in a language I don't understand. I wonder as I begin to jog through this lush island how is it that an entire country . . . indeed, much of Asia . . . has managed to side-step one of the great social ills of the West. From what I've learned talking to some of the English-speaking Koreans I've met, drug and alcohol abuse are simply not tolerated here. Sobriety is part of their culture. "With sobriety, anything is possible." That's the motto of Racing for Recovery. Maybe that help explains why countries like Korea did the seemingly impossible, transforming themselves in a few decades from rural, almost feudal societies ravaged by war into economic superpowers. They were sober.

The hours grind on. I want to stop. I want to go home. I want to throw up. But I keep going. I've learned to manage the pain somewhat, learned to shut out the distracting thoughts. Of course, it helps when you get a lift, which comes at the twenty-mile mark, when suddenly Jeremy—the nineteen-year-old Texan—bounds onto the course. "Hey, dude, how y'all doing?" he drawls.

"Jeremy!" I said, delighted to see a familiar face, much less one speaking English. "What happened?"

Jeremy explains that he didn't make the cutoff time on the bike. In the Ironman, there are mandatory time limits at each of the transitions. If you're not out of the water by two hours, you're out of the race. Ditto with the bike: If you can't finish the 112 miles ten hours after the start, you get the hook.

That's what happened to Jeremy. But he has the resilience and chipper attitude of a nineteen-year-old. He doesn't seem too fazed by coming all this way for a DNF (did not finish), and he's happy to accompany me the last ten kilometers of the run.

As we run into the soccer stadium for the finish, the cheers echoing into the night, the flashbulbs twinkling, I hear my name over the loudspeaker. "Todd Crandell of the United States," the announcer booms, in English. "The founder of Racing for Recovery." As I cross the finish line of my tenth Ironman, I think about the first nine, I think about home, and I think, with a bit of a shudder, about the old days. Then I recall something another Ironman said to me at the start of another race. "Todd, there is no place you would rather be today than here."

That wasn't true for most of my first twenty-five years on earth, but it is now—today and tomorrow; for the next ten Ironman triathlons; for the rest of my life.

10

Addict's Lessons Learned —and Advice for Parents

Years of addiction, years of sobriety, a lifetime spent either abusing or addressing the problem of drugs and alcohol: Believe me, I've learned a thing or two about what can go wrong . . . and how to make it go right. The road to sobriety is a long and difficult one, my friends, as you've seen from my own experience, but it can be successfully traveled. Here are some thoughts on what I've learned along the way—may these help guide you and your loved ones to the same destination.

* Recovery only works if you want it to.

If you are trying to get sober in order to please someone else, it's not going to work. I've tried that: I quit because my girlfriend Jenny begged me to; I quit because the judge ordered me to; I quit because my father threatened to kick me out of the house. Every time was short-lived: I ended up losing the girl, doing the time, getting the boot from the house. Why? Well, on one level, I did want to please these people. But the main reason I reverted to my addictive ways was that I really didn't want to stop for myself, first and foremost. I wanted to continue drinking and doing drugs, but I wanted to get these people off my back and avoid any consequences of my usage.

When I finally admitted to myself that I was going to die soon, and that I didn't want to die and the only way to prevent that was to quit—*that's* when I put down the drink. Willingly. Until you value your own life more than, or as much as, the lives around you, you're not going to be able to quit.

* Take full responsibility for your addiction and its consequences.

I don't want to hear anyone explaining their addiction away because of heredity. The idea that you're a drug addict or drunk because your father or your mother or your third cousin twice removed was also one is ridiculous. Sure, we know that your genes play a role in this. But it is not the fault of anyone or anything—certainly not some mindless strand of DNA . . . that you are an addict. Genes are responsible for an increased *risk* of addiction in many people who become addicts; they are not responsible for the addiction itself. *I* caused the miserable life I led for thirteen years. Yes, the fact that my mom and uncle were alcoholics is germane, but that's not what the academics would call "a necessary and sufficient condition." If anything, knowing my family history should have kept me away from the stuff. It was not my mom's fault, not my dad's fault, not my coach's fault, not the fault of the crowd I associated with or the school I attended. It was me. Each of us addicts has to face up to this fact. Once you can admit to this, once you choose to take responsibility for your actions, then you are on your way to long-term sobriety

* Redirect your addiction in a positive way.

A guy in a drug clinic once posed this question to me: "If you couldn't do another Ironman, would you go back to drinking?" "Heck no," was my response. Yes, I've willingly and gladly changed a positive addiction for a negative one, but I was sober for six years before I did my first Ironman. Training for these races has certainly become part of my recovery, but it is not the only thing keeping me from sliding back to the way I was thirteen years ago. No way.

That said, I do think my ten Ironman triathlons illustrate an important point about addiction—and ultimately one that can help many of us: Drug addicts are remarkably good at finding ways to feed their addiction. Think about it: We're creative, resourceful, imaginative, focused. We get results. Too bad those results often lead us to failures in education and at work, to jail, to disease, destroyed families, or an early grave. Still, that addictive energy, that determination, can be harnessed and redirected into a positive direction. When it is . . . watch out. I think my 10 Ironmans are an example of that—but so are the ex-addicts who've gone on to build businesses, write books, create music, lead ministries, have successful careers, have happy families. For many of them, it was a matter of taking the addictive aspects of their personality and channeling them in a different direction. So find that direction!

* **Build a strong support system.**

Family and friends may or may not have anything to do with the fact that you became an addict, but they can play a big role in your recovery. They and others—church, school, community—are essential for helping us get on and stay on the sober path. I'm often asked if I ever get the urge to use. Sure I do, but when I have those cravings (and I'm happy to say that as time goes, they are fewer and farther between), all I have to do is look at Madison, Skylar, Konor, and Mason and know what's really important. For others, it might be a phone call to another recovering addict or a support group. Whatever it is and whoever it involves, make your connection . . . build your support group.

* **Help yourself and others will help you.**

No one loves somebody who walks around hat in hand begging for money, especially when that somebody is a former drug addict who has probably already gone to the well too many times in the past. But if you help yourself, you will receive help from others. Getting sober triggered a cascade of positive outcomes in my life—I got back in shape, I returned to school, I found a great woman. I also repaired many of the relationships with friends and family that had been damaged during my drug years. I am sure one reason this happened was that people around me saw I was trying to help myself, and wanted to be part of it. Show the people in your life that you're working hard toward achieving your goal of sobriety and a new life. You won't have to ask for a helping hand—it will be offered.

* Take care of your body, and your heart will follow.

One reason I couldn't sit through some of the first support group meetings I attended was the fact that I was choking to death from all the cigarette smoke in the room. Why is it that addicts give up drugs and alcohol, only to kill themselves with cigarettes? Here's a suggestion: Instead of taking a drag, take a walk. Physical exercise is not only good for your heart and lungs, but also good for your head. Many studies have showed that symptoms stress, anxiety, even clinical depression can be alleviated through regular activity. You don't have to do triathlons or the Ironman. Even just a brisk, thirty-minute walk on most days of the week will help your mind—and body—a whole lot; certainly a whole lot more than a pot of coffee and a pack of cigarettes.

* *Believe* you can do it.

Remember that sobriety is not for those who need it but for those who choose to have it and work hard to maintain that sober lifestyle. If you want a better life for yourself, you will achieve it. I did it—so have hundreds of other addicts and alcoholics whom I've met or corresponded with over the years. It will take time, effort, and—a quality we addicts have to develop—patience. But I am living proof that it can be done; as are hundreds of my Racing for Recovery teammates, friends and support group members.

Sad to say, I also know many who lost hope, stopped trying, gave up on themselves. Some are dead now; the rest are desperate. The choice is yours. To paraphrase a song Mötley Crüe did not sing (it was actually the reggae musician Jimmy Cliff), "You can get it if you really want . . . you can get it if you really want. But you must try, try and try, try and try. You'll succeed at last."

I know you will, if a return to sobriety is truly in your heart.

Advice for Parents

Want to prevent your child from turning into a pre-recovery Todd Crandell? Here are some tips:

—Talk to your kids early and often about drugs. If you don't someone else will, and it may not be the message you want them to hear.

—Be a positive influence on your kids. Going out to a restaurant, having drinks with dinner, and then driving your family home, for example, does not set a good example.

—Get your kids involved in activities, sports, music, art. And be there to support these activities: Go to their soccer or baseball games; attend the school play or concert.

—Know your child's friends and their parents. Be aware of what they're doing, who they're hanging out with, what type of environment they're in.

—Recognize that drugs and alcohol are somewhere in your community, so do not be naive enough to think that your children will not come in contact with them, simply because of where you live or the economic level you have achieved. My dad runs a successful business and is a car enthusiast who belongs to the Porsche Club of Ohio. His son was an addict.

—Understand that virtually all adult addicts started down the road to addiction as youngsters, just as I did when I drank that first beer in the eighth grade, or as others did when they started smoking cigarettes at age ten. Be aware and if you see the danger signs, first try to deal with them yourself, in as positive and supportive way as you can. If that doesn't work in a relatively short time, get help—through the school, through your physician or through a social service agency—as soon as you can.

Maybe, despite all your precautions, you suspect your child is using. What are the warning signs? Personality changes, changes in eating habits, changes in activity habits, changes in his or her group of friends (and they happen to be friends you never get to meet). Any of these changes in and of itself may be no cause for alarm; kids obviously go through changes—that's what growing up is. But when the sum total of what might otherwise be normal or explainable changes adds up to something that doesn't smell right, there may be a problem. Now is the time to begin seeking some form of counseling or treatment. Don't just hope they'll stop or "grow out of it"—because they may not.

I hope that turns out not to be the case; that you will have to read no further than this; that you can continue to be a parent who is playing "prevent defense" against substance abuse, as opposed to dealing with a real problem. If you are the parent of an addict, however, you have my sympathies. I saw the toll my addiction took on my father and stepmom, and I admit it's only in recent years that these relationships have been repaired. Some of the scars may never heal. Still, there are things you can do to both help and hinder your child's recovery.

The cardinal rule for parents of addicts is this: If you are doing something to further that addiction, stop it. If you are doing something to help the recovery, keep doing it. Example: Your son calls and says, "I got arrested for drunk driving for the third time, I'm in jail, come get me." Your response should be, "I'll see you when you get out." I know it sounds cold and heartless; it's not. It's the ultimate form of what's so often called "tough love," and with good reason: This is one of the toughest emotional situations a parent can deal with. And it's counterintuitive. Your gut instinct is to want to help. But in a situation like that, you are not. You are essentially helping to feed his addiction.

On the flip side, if your child calls and says, "I need a ride to a support group meeting" or "I've decided to go back to college, can you help me pay for it?" or "I'm struggling right now, can you come and talk to me?" then the answer is yes, yes, yes.

Remember: they've got to get to a point where the addictive life they're leading is so distasteful that they want to stop. That's addiction and recovery in a nutshell: The addict has had enough of the life he or she is leading, wants something better, and is willing to do what it takes to achieve that goal. When this happens, you can have a vital and positive part to play. Now there are many things you can do—help fund the recovery program, join your child at support group meetings, get any medical help he or she may need, and above all provide "soft" (as opposed to tough) love and support.

At this point, when your child is making a genuine effort to recover, you can and should say yes. Until then, to use the clichéd drug advice of decades ago, you're going to have steel yourself and just say "no" to aiding and abetting your child's continued use of drugs and alcohol.

My children.

Todd Crandell is the founder and executive director of Racing for Recovery. He lives in Sylvania, Ohio. He has completed ten Ironman triathlons. Please visit **www.racingforrecovery.com**.

John Hanc is the author of five books on fitness and running. He is a long-time fitness and active-sports writer for *Newsday* and a frequent contributor to *Runner's World;* his work has appeared in many publications, including *AARP Bulletin, The Boston Globe Sunday Magazine, Men's Fitness, Playboy, Yoga Journal,* and *Smithsonian.* Hanc also teaches writing and journalism at the New York Institute of Technology in Old Westbury, New York. A long-time competitive distance runner, Hanc completed his twenty-first career marathon at Marine Corps in Washington, D.C. in October 2005.